Praise for
The Bad Girls Club

"This powerful book is a must-read for any professional seeking to overcome personal challenges while maintaining focus and drive in their career. Ms. Marginot brilliantly illustrates how recovery from addiction not only leads to personal freedom but also strengthens leadership, decision-making, and resilience in business. This is more than a story of recovery; it's a compass guiding you to unleash your full personal and professional capabilities."

—Tim Ryan, thought leader, Dope to Hope LLC

"A professional finding her passion, a writer finding her voice, and a leader finding her calling. In this candid and powerful book, Karen shares her transformative journey of recovery from addiction, offering hope, practical insights, and a blueprint for personal and professional growth. Beyond just a story of sobriety, this inspiring work demonstrates how overcoming addiction can strengthen leadership, decision-making, and resilience in all aspects of one's life. With raw honesty and profound wisdom, Karen shows how recovery is not only a path to freedom but also a gateway to rediscovering joy, purpose, and

fulfillment. A must-read for anyone navigating their own recovery or seeking to unlock their full potential in both life and career."
—Declan Lynch, business executive, nonprofit board director, and former active-duty military leadership instructor

"With unflinching honesty and profound compassion, this transformative memoir delves deep into the heart of addiction and recovery, illuminating the complex emotional landscape of healing. The author's raw and intimate narrative goes beyond mere survival, exploring the profound personal metamorphosis that occurs when one confronts the deepest roots of dependency. More than a story of breaking free from substance abuse, this book is a powerful testament to human resilience, self-discovery, personal redemption, and the remarkable capacity to transform and rebuild one's life with authenticity and purpose."
—Jen Marples, host, *The Jen Marples Show*, and founder, the Jen Marples Agency

"Karen Marginot's journey is a testament to the power of hard work and unrelenting self-discovery. As a friend, parent, teammate, leadership coach, and now an author, Ms. Marginot brings the same determination and honesty to this memoir that she has demonstrated in every facet of life. Her deep excavation of the past—getting to the roots of causes and conditions—is an inspiring blueprint for anyone seeking fulfillment and success in their personal or professional lives.

"The stories of 'Location Unknowns' hit close to home, reminding us of the chaos addiction can bring, not only to individuals but to the teams and organizations around them.

"Most importantly, this book is a powerful reminder that 'acceptance is the answer to all my problems today.' Ms. Marginot doesn't just share a story; she illuminates a path forward for all of us. This is more than a memoir; it's a call to action, a guide, and a source of hope."

—Earl L. Murphy, Enterprise account executive, president of Soberforce, Salesforce

"In this inspiring book, Marginot takes readers through the raw and transformative process of recovery, offering hope, guidance, and practical insights for anyone with substance use disorder (commonly known as addiction). It's not just a journey of recovery—it's about rediscovering joy, purpose, and true fulfillment. A refreshingly candid book for those on the path of recovery and for professionals working in this space."

—Eliza Zarka, director, Global Recovery Initiatives Foundation

"*The Bad Girls Club* is a compelling exploration of the often-tumultuous journey from childhood to adulthood. It delves deep into the complexities of family relationships, particularly the dynamics between mothers and daughters.

"Karen's story is a powerful testament to the ways individuals cope with mental anguish, particularly through the lure of drugs and alcohol. The author deftly illustrates how these choices, while often seen as escapes, can lead to even deeper pain. Yet the book also offers a glimmer of hope, emphasizing the importance of confronting and gently sitting with our emotions as a pathway to recovery.

"*The Bad Girls Club* is a thought-provoking read that challenges us to confront our pasts and embrace the journey toward self-discovery and healing."

—Holly Mayes, author of *Dream, Girl: A Memoir*

"*The Bad Girls Club* is a courageous tale of one woman's journey to sobriety. Raw, heartbreaking, and profoundly honest, it shines with generosity and resilience, offering hope and inspiration to anyone seeking redemption and the strength to transform their life."

—Isabelle Wettergren, senior consultant, Workplace Division, R1 Learning

"A transparent journey through the struggles of addiction, this book offers deeply personal reflections and sensemaking."

—Caroline Walsh, author of
*Fairly Smooth Operator:
My Life Occasionally at the Tip of the Spear*

The Bad Girls Club: Promises of a Spirituality-Based Recovery
by Karen Marginot

© Copyright 2025 Karen Marginot

ISBN 979-8-88824-596-5

Library of Congress Control Number: 2024920785

All rights reserved. No part of this publication may be reproduced, stored in a retrieval system, or transmitted in any form or by any means—electronic, mechanical, photocopy, recording, or any other—except for brief quotations in printed reviews, without the prior written permission of the author.

Edited by Miranda Dillon
Cover Design by Catherine Herold

Published by

3705 Shore Drive
Virginia Beach, VA 23455
800-435-4811
www.koehlerbooks.com

THE BAD GIRLS CLUB

*Promises of a
Spirituality-Based Recovery*

KAREN MARGINOT

VIRGINIA BEACH
CAPE CHARLES

For Ryan and Anton. This is the beginning of my path that brought me to you.

Contents

Author's Note 11
Foreword 15

Part 1 20
    A Knock at the Door 21
    All the Days and Nights Before 27
    Universal Intervention 43
    Dropping the Bags 62
    Compassion 102
    Forgiveness 119

Part 2 125
    Changelings 126
    Yogaville and the Lotus Shrine 140
    Returning 147
    Miracles 157
    Landing 172
    The Trifecta of Ts 182

Part 3 190
    Velveteen 191
    The Bad Girls Club 193
    Coming Home to Acceptance 216

Acknowledgments 227
Resources 229
Citations 232

Author's Note

This is a memoir, much of which is recalled from an increasingly faulty memory from decades past, and many of those memories are clouded and colored by chemicals of various natures. So, it's very much an imperfect recollection. These, however, are the stories I've adopted as my history—my personal history—none of which I would change. They've built the path through woods and fields, deep darkness and stunning light, upon which my feet were planted and still follow today. I want to recognize and acknowledge the tremendous privileges I have been granted throughout my life: an intact family of origin, economic means, and the support of friends, community, and family. My family is like most American families and, I would guess, families across the globe: wanting the best for their children and trying their best to deliver that. Complicated, flawed, well-intentioned, working through their own stuff. Human.

Most names have been changed to protect those who journeyed alongside me. A few characters have been combined as a composite to simplify your orientation to the events described. None of the literary techniques leveraged in these pages are intended for deceitful purposes; rather, they were used in service to the stories offered to you.

A message for the male readers who may have opened

this book: You are welcome here too. You may have been drawn to the title because you know a bad girl or two who's struggling. Maybe it's your girlfriend, your wife, your sister, your mother, or a colleague. Maybe it's even you. You're welcome here. Although this is written from a woman's point of view, the inner experiences defy gender. As my counselor told me, "Listen for the feelings."

I am surrounded by courageous women. Here are some of our stories, and some of mine, from when I was young to when I came into my own. May you find hope, humor, and experience you can learn from in these pages.

I was born with what I call "a custom set of legs." Hip dysplasia, found a bit late, resulted in surgeries and confinement in body casts and braces on my legs. I couldn't really play the same as other kids. My mother must have read to me; I don't have any real memories of that, sadly, but she's an avid reader, and my father was working and in school, so it was just the two of us alone in a little apartment in Alexandria, Virginia. She must have introduced me to the magical escape and wonder of books because, before I knew it, I was devouring four or five at a time.

Growing up in the sixties and seventies, there was so much time spent in unremarkable ways. We were the latchkey kids, the ones raised in ways Social Services would now deem neglect. But it gave us choice and boredom and risks and freedom and outdoors and honeybees in my hair and cops and robbers, kickball in the street, running between cars and bikes. Biking for hours and hours and hours without helmets and cell phones and any way of an adult knowing where we were or who we were with. An American treasure of a storyteller, Garrison Keillor, spoke of his childhood as a time when children didn't know their father's professions and freely roamed their neighborhoods, the woods, and thickets in their towns. Imagined executions took place in those woods, conducted by ruthless pirates and robbers. It was a time of endless imagination and play, where all sides of justice and injustice were examined and enacted, and losses and victories abounded. It was electronic-free and innocent. It was childhood.

My favorite place was in a white wicker rocking chair on the second-floor screened-in porch of our home, surrounded by trees. With a stack of books on the side table, I'd drift away to places far and near, fantastical and frightening, always with an expanding sense of exploration. I don't know how long I sat in that rocker, how many summers I drifted away there, but if you asked me now, I'd say it was my entire childhood.

It seemed, without question, that I would become a writer. I couldn't think of anything more powerful, more impactful, or more purposeful than writing down stories and giving them to the world. And yet it's taken me decades, many decades, of traveling down my own journey to come home to my voice.

My path to full integration and contentment didn't start there, but I'm grateful it's where I've landed. From such an unwilling, scared, addicted beginning, I was able to heal so much trauma, shame, and everything that grew from that dark landscape. From dropping out of college—lost and terrified of everything—I learned how to embrace the wise framework offered by the Twelve Steps to create a life filled with love, big courage, professional achievement, gratitude, financial stability, and deep contentment. I'm sharing my story with anyone who feels they don't quite measure up, those secretly afraid they aren't as brave as they should be or that they lack the kind of authenticity or character they see so many people around them demonstrate so (seemingly) effortlessly. My secret fears took me into poor choices and through hard addictions to alcohol, drugs, men, sex, food, terrifying, dark depressions, and years of heart-pounding anxiety. But I've come out of all of that, and you can too. Join me in the bad girls' club and hold a light for the women coming after you.

Foreword

Addiction is a snake that coils around you, and it is a hard one to release once it has its fangs in you.

It was only during my five hundredth time trying to stop drinking that I read a statistic. Well, rather, I heard it as I was listening to yet another *How to Stop Alcohol* book on Audible. There had been a few of those over the years.

"It takes ten to thirty years to become dependent on alcohol."

That shook me. I wasn't dependent. I wasn't addicted. *Was I?* I just liked it. A lot. I was a "social drinker," and I had been drinking since I was fourteen. That was three decades plus a few years. Fourteen was the age I first went to a party and got blackout drunk on shots with my crew. Or was it sambuca? I forget, along with the many other nights like that over the next few years. My parents had a fully stocked bar in the house and allowed us a glass of wine as teens over a meal.

"It's a good way to learn to drink moderately," they said as they finished a scotch and then a bottle or two of wine with a meal every night. "They do that in Europe." They never got too angry when we teens took the entire bottle of vodka during a sleepover. It was a bit of a lark. Silly kids.

Alcohol was *fun*. It was the way we celebrated, partied, relaxed, and went out. It was also how we spent lazy Sunday lunches, long weekends at the river, evenings on the beach, sundowners, and late nights in clubs. At my twenty-first birthday party, I drank so much during the afternoon buildup that I threw up and passed out at 7 p.m.—before the guests even arrived. Everyone thought it was hilarious, and it was laughed about for weeks and retold at countless reunions with friends. I had alcohol poisoning and couldn't get out of bed for two days.

During our thirties, it was how we rewarded ourselves after a long, hard day of parenting. In our forties, it was just what we did at night over dinner. But it was becoming less fun. Not the drinking! That part was fun. What wasn't was the longer hangovers and restless nights that took their toll.

It wasn't a problem in my life; it just made me sluggish and tired the next day. I reeled into my third decade of "social drinking," along with most of my friends.

But something strange happened. When I was writing my last book, *Love and Above: A journey through Shamanism, Coma and Joy*, I had to go through my old diaries to check some facts and dates. I sat on the floor with my life record in front of me, and for the first time, I saw a pattern. From nineteen to forty-six, one thing was repeated again and again in those personal notes, in black and white.

"Hungover."

"I hate alcohol."

Every New Year, my resolutions started the same over those three decades.

"Stop drinking."

There had been entire years when I had done just that. There was a two-year dry spell in my thirties (high five to that!). But it had always snuck back into my life. Each time, it was nastier to me, and I was older, and the hangovers were worse. Even two glasses of wine meant a fuzzy head the next day.

"Not worth it," my diary read then. "Stop."

I had watched friends who were "proper addicts" over the years. Some kicked addictions hard and fast in their twenties. They were the heroes and the brave ones. But most others kept going quietly, never with a "big problem," just a social drinker or using party drugs only. They managed it behind work, jobs, lives, trance festivals, big nights out, and busy families. These were the high-functioning ones, and it was "not a problem."

But addiction is a quiet thief. It robs you. What it takes away is honesty, self-development, and rich intimacy. Your personal favorite becomes your friend, companion, and source of joy. Glass of wine at 6 p.m.? Then the music comes on, and let's cook a great meal. Another few glasses over dinner, and then off to bed. Another restless night, more visits to the loo, and then up at 6 a.m. again for work, life, and parenting.

When I put all those diaries away, finished my book, and went on a book tour, this lingering, horrible realization was still with me. It was a slow-burn decision, but I knew what I had to do.

It was no surprise to me when I woke up one morning after another dinner with a few bottles, with a single and clear thought: *I am done with alcohol.*

It had taken me thirty years to get there.

I met Karen that very year on the island of Lamu, an exotic and otherworldly place in East Africa off the coast of Kenya. We both were at a literary and music festival, which was rich with music, drinks, and spectacular people. Karen stood out of the crowd of hipsters and fashionistas as the cocktails swirled. It was a week of parties as we stepped onto magical dhow boats and sailed out on sunset cruises.

Karen stood out with her bad girl full-arm tattoo, sparkling eyes, and buoyant being.

I watched how everyone was drawn to her and her clear thinking, her kind words, and her engagement with people. She was positive, a great listener, filled with joy, and simply so much fun. I also noticed she didn't drink. I was looking for people who were "clean" as I was battling to have fun without my faithful handmaiden of joy—white wine.

I watched her laugh hugely, dance late, and fill the room with positivity. When she shared her staggering story of sobriety with the group of writers, I immediately wanted to be her friend. You will too when you read this book.

The story you are about to read is radical and real. In it, she shares how she careened into her twenties with booze, drugs, and reckless out-of-control behavior. She was drinking and drugging, living with a coke-dealing boyfriend, and crashing her life before she finally bottomed out.

Karen was lucky, in a sense. Her boss saw what was really going on and supported her into rehab. She was lucky because her addiction changed her life—in a good way. Nobody wants to be in a recovery center in your twenties. Nobody wants to be an addict or give up that high, and Karen's rebellious nature had her breaking down the rehab walls. But she was lucky because that intervention changed her life and opened a door into her spirit and soul that was to grow and grow.

This story will grab you from the second you start, and it will not let you go. I literally could not put it down. It will also challenge what you think is a "normal woman" living a "normal life" and show you the clawing power of addiction. It will show you the courage of faith it takes to not just kick it but to go on living sober and clean.

Getting clean was just the start of this journey, and she struggled to fill that hole inside in the years that followed.

She confesses that she feared that hole would always remain.

It is also really interesting that getting clean is not enough. If we want to grow and live a rich and rewarding life, there is work to be done, and her work was long and hard. Karen's authentic story takes us through the real hard work of growth. She describes her world orbiting around a trifecta of Ts—trade (jobs), testosterone (men), and treasure (money)—and how she judged her self-worth based on how she fared in each of those areas.

This is a big journey you are going to take with her. It will make you gasp, and it will most certainly make you laugh. Her sense of humor is so acute and rich that you will be rolling on the floor, wanting to call Karen up for a coffee and a good chat.

Sarah Bullen is a multi-published author, international writing coach, and literary agent. Founder of The Writing Room and Kent Literary, she runs writing workshops and mentorships. Her recent books include *Write Your Book in 100 Days: Stop Mucking About & Just Write Your Book* and *Love and Above: a journey into shamanism, coma and joy*.

Her latest book, *The Other Side: Journeys into Mysticism, Magic and Near Death*, gathers riveting and radical stories of people who have crossed to the "other side" or those who can contact it.

Part 1

bo·dy / [Honesty]

"There is nothing as glorious and terrible as living a human existence."
—Karen Marginot

"We have to dare to be ourselves, however frightening or strange that self may prove to be."
—May Sarton, *Journal of a Solitude*

A Knock at the Door

Nearly forty years ago, I descended into hell, where I knew I belonged.

Three-fifteen on a moonless September morning. Driving home in my sporty red Audi 2005, I grabbed the wheel with both hands, pulled hard to the left, floored the gas pedal, and shut my eyes. The car shot up to 110 mph, hit the guardrail hard, bounced, right tires catching on the embankment, and flipped, spinning into a roll again and again and again down the interstate. Metal and glass grinding and popping until the car lurched back onto four broken wheels, and everything stopped.

Silence.

Years later, after decades of recovery, this is what I told my sons: alcohol is a sneaky bitch. If you've got an addiction in your genetic makeup, she'll find it and flip it on. She'll get in you, down deep, and then reach up and grab you by the throat from the inside before you know what's happening, and then you're done. We have so much family history in this space of addiction. The odds of you navigating alcohol safely and without consequence, I told them, are slim to none, so choose carefully.

I honestly wish someone had told me that.

I don't know if it would have changed anything—maybe. But I know for a fact that once you hear something, you can't unhear it. And alarms may have gone off in the back of my mind.

At least, that's what I'd hoped for my sons.

I didn't know I was an alcoholic or an addict. I knew that most of the time, I could drink a lot. More than most people I knew, and I rarely had hangovers. I thought alcohol was the one thing that was keeping me together, keeping me from losing my shit. There were a whole lot of other drugs in between the time I started drinking at what I joke is "the drinking age for Irish Catholic drunks," age eleven, and the time the collision course I was on landed me in a treatment center at twenty-three. I came into my alcoholic prime during the Reagan era's War On Drugs, and so I knew drugs are bad, *mkay*? But *alcohol*? I was not keen on navigating life without it; in fact, I knew in my bones that would be a very bad idea indeed.

But when I started drinking in the basement of my former home, inhabited by a new family with a daughter my age, I didn't know I was flipping a switch inside of me that could no longer be turned off. Like nearly every alcoholic I've known, from that first sip of tequila, I felt "fixed" in a way that felt life-changing. I was astonished that alcohol was illegal for me to drink. I thought it instantly healed everything inside of me that was broken. With alcohol in me, I no longer felt *alone, scared, confused, lost, anxious, terrified, angry, hopeless, damaged, broken.*

My experiences in my body were all so painful, starting with the postsurgical terror during my first night in a hospital, alone in the dark, with deep pulsing throbs swallowing my body. The sting from a bee as I curiously sniffed a flower. Pain and humiliation as I fell, over and over, knees collapsing, body crumbling, classmates laughing in bullying delight. Rejection, disdain, and punishment at home. Bones broken: wrists, clavicle, knees. And the assaults—unwelcome tongues shoved down my throat. Raped at the start of college, another sexual assault in my home in Washington, none of which I recognized as *assault* or *rape* or even as a *crime victim*. I assumed each event was entirely my fault, so I didn't tell anyone.

Lying became a crucial survival technique, as did the cigarettes I stole from my mother's purse and the whiskey I drank after school. As a toddler, I stole vanilla extract; I craved the alcohol even as I grimaced from its terrible taste. In my teens, I turned to whiskey, Marlboro's, and unfiltered Camels, graduating to pot, speed, hash, and pills, landing firmly and fashionably in the eighties cocaine madness and anything else offered that didn't involve a needle.

Saints suffer, I learned in Catholic schools. Suffering was the cleanse through which you found God, or God found you. But as each year passed, I drifted and ran farther until not even God could intervene.

Some mornings, I woke with a feeling from a dream, just eluding me on the edge of my memory, something important. On days that began with that elusive itch, I thought about all the things I knew and everything I still needed to know.

My education spanned Catholic elementary school, public

middle, and high school. Before I was midway through high school, I was a daily after-school drinker, always finding a steady supply in the living room armoire. My cousin first introduced me to pot, which I gladly continued smoking with my classmates in their basements, in the woods, and in field parties. But my reliable access to alcohol negated any desire for me to pursue buying pot. I just used drugs when they were available.

The high school friends I had numbered fewer than the fingers on my hand. The corridors were filled with kids who, like me, had grown up in the neighborhood, their families rotating through military service assignments. I made sure I knew people from each clique: the freaks, jocks, geeks, art geeks, the popular girls. I knew everyone and could blend in with most, but I didn't belong to any group. My closest friend, a year ahead of me in school, drifted away as her popularity soared, breaking my heart. Feeling a desperate void, I developed close relationships with Mary, a perennial homecoming court member and cheerleader, and June, another cheerleader and student government member. Maria, whose shadow I stayed behind in middle school, had disappeared. Not knowing what happened to her, I made up a story that she had run away to Richmond, where she was kidnapped and killed or sold into sex trafficking. What remaining friends I'd had in middle school distanced from me after my rumor spread.

As we had done for years, June and I continued to walk together to and from school. We had long talks about everything: her parents' divorce, my mother's anger, school, boys. "I don't know how you stay so happy," I mused one afternoon. It was true; no matter what happened to her, June remained steadfastly happy, grounded, and grateful. She was sunny, always smiling.

"It's Jesus," June said, her eyes beaming. "He's always with me. He understands everything, and he's truly my best friend."

I was dumbstruck. I'd never known June to be religious, and yet here she was, simply stating that she had a relationship with Jesus.

"Do you go to church?" I asked, unsure of how to proceed.

"No, not really," she responded. "My mom introduced me to Jesus and taught me how to pray. I pray and talk to him all day now! And she teaches me about his life and how to know him. We don't go to church, but we read and talk about it at home. You could talk to her about him if you want to. I'm sure she'd love it if you did," she added encouragingly.

My mind drew a blank. I didn't know how to respond. *June is so happy*, I thought. But I didn't want to go to church. I'd had enough of religion in Catholic school, and none of that had made any sense to me. I wasn't sure I understood what June meant about *talking about it at home*. My family didn't talk about anything, and the thought of talking about Jesus seemed too unreal. It felt vulnerable, and I wasn't sure why. Realizing that I'd stayed quiet too long, I uncomfortably said, "That's really nice. I'll think about talking to your mom."

In my dream, I saw June slowly waving to me from a driveway. I walked toward her, and she was gone. Everything melted into shades of green: apple, sage, celery, fern, juniper. I walked between dense, dark, arching woods down a dark, mossy dirt path until the trees arched away to my left and right. Before me was an expanse of emerald-green grass. Kelly-green moss-covered slabs of stone continued the path from the dirt driveway to an enormous Southern colonial home, complete with Greek Revival pillars segmenting a wraparound porch. Everything was dreamy shades of green—the porch, the pillars, the house, the roof, and the sky. Silently, I continued walking and stepped up onto the porch. A low rocking swing bench, suspended by a metallic green chain, invited me to sit. In slow motion, it moved with the breeze that gently nudged the treetops this way and that. No sound. Everything was still and moving so slowly, shades of emerald lying before me.

All the Days and Nights Before

At the end of each workday at a regional advertising agency, where I had just been hired as a proofreader, I stopped anywhere to avoid my lonely, sparse apartment. It wasn't my home; it was just a place where I dumped my stuff and slept when I had no other choice. Restless, I walked up Fifteenth Street to the Post Pub, a salty institution in the DC news and ad hack circles.

I sat at the bar and ordered a Heineken. Another. Still restless and irritated for no clear reason, I started to settle in. Unsure of what I was looking for, I ordered onion rings and another Heiny. Some random guy sitting next to me chatted me up, bought me a gin and tonic, and got friendly with my thighs. *He's kind of smarmy*, I thought. *But he's nice enough. He's still buying me drinks, so why not hang out with him?* A couple of rounds later, we walked out, headed back down the street, and landed at Chelsea's. Music was blaring, and the gravelly-voiced Joe Strummer belted out "Rock the Casbah." Bodies dancing, dark, close, some slamming into each other, and that was okay. BOOM, BOOM, BA BOOM, BOOM. The base pounded. Pointing vaguely toward the back, I yelled, "Bathroom" and ditched the guy, splitting through the back door into an alley and back down M Street toward Poseurs. I always ended up there. The doorman let me in, and I ran into Pat. His voice, smooth as silk, welcomed me with a "Hey, baby." He handed me a pill.

"You okay, girl? Take this. It's good."

"What is it?"

"Just take it. You'll like it." I swallowed the pill with a swig from his drink.

A little unsteady on my feet, my shoulder brushing against the wall, I walked down the cattle chute hallway and turned left into the dark club, bright, blinking string lights shining down from the ceiling. The dance floor was packed, dancers colliding with punks standing at the bar across the room, drinks occasionally splashing. I looked around and instantly spotted Sam. She was the blond, and I was the brunette. Her edgy, swingy, blunt-cut bangs framed her wide eyes, the lights framing her height in an aural glow, giving her plenty of length to weave a path through the crowd. Lifting two pitchers of Long Island Iced Teas high, she laughingly made her way to our table in the bay window, up on the stage. *She's the brave one*, I thought. *No fear.*

Just last week, she grabbed my hand and pulled me outside and into a van, yelling, "Let's go to Canada!" And off we went, without a second thought. I panicked as the van pulled away from the curb and turned over the Key Bridge and onto the GW Parkway, headed north to Maryland, pulled by the draw of Montreal. My anxiety rose to meet her level of fearlessness, and they went to battle.

"But I have to work!" I protested. "I can't do this. You have to turn around. You have to let me out."

"Oh, don't worry about it," Sam purred. "We'll be back before you know it, and they won't even miss you." She put her arm around me and kissed me on the cheek. "C'mon! Let's have some fun!" She winked at the guys in the front and pulled a pipe out of her pocket. "Fill it up, boys," she sassed as she handed the pipe to the one riding shotgun. He smiled and filled the pipe with weed. Lighting the pipe and pulling a long hit, he handed it back to Sam. "Here, baby," she said to me. "Take a little pull and relax. We're going on an adventure."

I smiled, remembering that trip. I never would have done that without her. "Gimme some of that," I said, pointing to the Long Islands Sam put on the table. The drinks went down just like iced tea on a hot summer's day, and I realized how thirsty I was. I downed another. Someone broke out a vial and passed it around. The music pulsed through the floor, into the soles of my feet, up my legs, wrapped around my hips, shot up through my stomach and back, and slid up my throat and neck. My eyes closed. I swayed as the room drifted away, leaving nothing but the bass and the sound of my breathing.

The energy shifted, and I felt warm happiness pulsing down my body. I opened my eyes and saw him just as he saw me. His eyes widened, and he burst into a huge smile.

"My love," he shouted above the noise, and the crowd parted for him as he strode toward me. I leaned back in my chair, giddy and giggling with anticipation. Still grinning, Thomas took one last long step, opened his arms wide, and scooped me up and out of the chair. I wrapped my legs around his waist. Simultaneously, we buried our faces in each other's necks, breathing each other in. He smelled so good. Like home. He was my home, and I didn't want to let go.

"How was your week, baby? Miss me?"

"My week was hard! You know I hate it when you leave. I'm so happy you're back. Please don't leave me again. You know how much I hate it when you go."

"I don't want to fight now, baby. Let's just have a good time and enjoy the night." His eyes grew darker. Hints of a smile at the corners, but a far-off storm moved closer, and I backed off.

Thomas left me every month for a week to visit his other

girlfriend in New York, Jane. He said he met her at Poseur's the same night he met me and instantly loved us both. I asked him all the time who was the "other woman," and he couldn't tell, said it changed all the time. It killed me, and I avoided thinking about it, managing to stay happily in love until it was time for him to leave again. The rage that filled me while he was gone grew in intensity and nearly always coincided with my period. Spiking hormones mixed with scorned love was more than I could bear. To get through the pain and the waiting, I sought out oblivion and revenge with another man, usually Pat, a skilled lover, always waiting in the wings. But while Pat was steady, sweet, and generous, he wasn't as intoxicating as Thomas. A constant desire for Thomas ran through me, masking and overriding the emotional devastation that visited me every four weeks.

"What are you drinking tonight, my love? Let me get you another." Thomas quickly returned with a Black Russian, which I loved because it went well with the 1950s silk black prom dress I was wearing, complete with multiple strands of rhinestone necklaces, a spiky steel bracelet, and Doc Martens combat boots. It was a good look.

The night was the same as all others in the club. Some kid we called Little Boy came to our table for a visit. Thomas broke out a rock of coke and shared it around the table of regulars. We danced together, individually, wildly through the video lineup of the late seventies punk greats. We egged Sam on as she hunted for that evening's conquest to bed. When Sid Vicious ended the night with his hearty rendition of "My Way," we knew the bar was closed, the lights were about to come on, and it was time to head home. Hopping on the back of Thomas's Suzuki Katana, we whipped between traffic back over the bridge spanning the Potomac River, raced down Route 50, and parked at Thomas's mother's home.

"Shh," he reminded me as we snuck into his basement apartment. "Remember that my mom doesn't want you here, but as long as you're quiet, you can stay as long as you want."

Throughout the night, people came by, knocking softly on the basement window, looking to buy weed and cocaine. Thomas silently conducted his business while I lay waiting in bed. By the time I woke in the morning, he was gone to his day job. I stayed behind, quiet, waiting for him to return. Resentment laid small foundations in my gut, brick by brick, thought by thought. *How could he leave me stuck here for endless hours in silence? Why didn't his mom like me? How could he leave me each month to see another woman? How could he cheat on me? Why did I stand for it? Why didn't he love me enough to leave her?* I paced circles in his room, getting angrier by the hour. The unanswered questions swirled, and my silent fuming smoldered, igniting a small flame of fear, panic, and resentment taking shape as a funnel in my stomach, twisting, rising through my diaphragm, filling my chest, tightening my throat until I was choking, choking for breath.

I tore through his chest of drawers, looking for weed, a bottle, a rock of cocaine, anything to dispel the tornado within me. Finding nothing, I threw open the door to his closet and tore through the space, clothing flying off hangers, discarding each piece on a pile on the floor, box tops flipping open, my fingers flying through contents until I uncovered his stash. *Ahhhh.* Rocks and rocks and rocks of cocaine appeared before me, and dark angels sang in my head. *Glorious*! I breathed deeply, eager to break one down. Calmer, with great anticipation, I turned and pulled over a record album. Sneaking into the bathroom, I grabbed a razor blade. Returning to his room, I sat beside the closet door and pulled over the stash box. A little giddy now, thinking, *There's so much here for me!* I picked up a smaller rock, placed it carefully in the box top, laid that on the record album cover, and shaved the cocaine down into powder. Rolling a twenty-dollar bill, I bent over and snorted two lines. The rush hit me hard, and then I relaxed. I could relax. I snorted two more lines, the bitter taste running down the back of my throat. *I'll tell him what I did. He owed me this for leaving me with nothing, trapped here. It's the price he pays for that*, I thought. It made sense to me, and it will make sense to him. *He'll understand.* I finished the rock, opened a bag of pills, swallowed two with a leftover shot of whiskey left on the nightstand, put on Aerosmith's *Toys in the Attic*, and crawled back into bed, curling up into the waves of the music.

Days and nights followed the same pattern. Waiting. Then, days and nights cocooning in his room, filled with wild, hungry lovemaking, drinking, pills, weed, hash, cocaine, and, for him, heroin. He always offered, but I drew the line at shooting speedballs. Every night at the club, every night, the same mix. And then three weeks later, he left me again.

Too drunk and stoned to drive, I laid on my side on the floor of my apartment, alone in my underwear, watching the nightly formation of roaches creep out from the baseboard in front of the kitchen. Carefully, I positioned a heaping spoonful of bright-blue boric acid and slowly dribbled a few grains of the crystallized killer over the first roach. It stopped, and the line of followers split to continue around its fallen leader. Fascinated, I scooped another spoonful and sprinkled it over the entire line.

"Incoming," I whispered as I slowly poured more and more acid on the infestation. I watched through slitted eyes as the roaches squirmed to escape their blue death. I spread the granules around in a wide perimeter, containing the offending intruders, and methodically rained down more poison. *How long will it take them to die?* I wondered. For a moment, I considered whether I felt bad for them, if what I was doing was cruel. No. I realized I felt nothing for them, and I actually felt nothing inside at all. I slowly dribbled acid granules over the suffering mass of indestructible beings.

Waking up, I didn't know where I was . . . again. I must have gone out, but I couldn't remember anything. This was somebody's bed. Yellow sheets, sort of faux silk, sweaty. My clothes were on the floor. *Fuck—what time was it?* My head screamed for more sleep, some relief. Everything hurt; small bruises threatened to take over the inside of my arms. Nauseous, I wondered and didn't want to know what had happened last night. I scanned the messy room—piles of clothes flung carelessly over a chair, a small dirty window, and a dank smell of mold. The window was positioned high up on the wall, and I thought I was in a basement apartment. Alone. I quickly dressed and walked out of the one-room apartment, past the kitchenette, and out the door. A few cars lined the street. Mostly Maryland plates. *Good, okay*, so I was somewhere in Maryland. I realized I was in the middle of a block, and most of the traffic was moving to my left. Looking down that way, I saw what I thought looked like the big M metro sign. Relief poured over me when I found a metro card with a few bucks left on it in the side pocket of my purse. I could get out and back to work; it had to be near the start of the workday. I trotted toward the metro and figured I would deal with finding my car later.

Pausing just outside the building entrance back on Fifteenth Street, I pressed my button-down shirt over my skirt to stretch out the wrinkles. Leaving that apartment in Maryland, I hadn't had time to go home to change, and I hoped no one would notice I was wearing the same clothes as yesterday. Taking a deep breath, I strode into the office building, faking confidence with every step, opened the door on floor five, and walked past the receptionist without saying a word. She stared at me harshly. I got to my seat and saw a handwritten note on a message page taped to the phone: "See me as soon as you get in. David."

I stopped by his secretary's desk, and she nodded that I could go in. Nervously, I opened the door to David's office. Leaning over his left shoulder was Pauline Goldman, the HR director. David looked up.

"Woah," he said, shocked. "You look terrible. Ooof, and you smell like a bar. Wait—are you drunk right now?"

"N-n-no sir, I'm not drunk," I stammered.

"David," Pauline interjected, stopping his rant. She pointed to the chair in front of the desk.

"Karen, we've called you in here because you're being released. That means that you are being fired for cause, and you cannot resign. Including today, you've been late to work over fifty percent of the time. And because you've only worked here for three weeks, we are under no obligation to pay out any severance to you. You'll have fifteen minutes to collect your things and leave the building. On a personal note, and to David's point, girl, you are a hot mess. You need to get yourself together."

I knew I was a mess. I didn't need David or Pauline or anyone else, for that matter, to tell me that. I knew I smelled; I was starting to look janky all the time. I was a total failure; I'd been fired now from every single ad agency in the DC market. Total failure. I knew I had somehow lost the ability to hide my shit. I couldn't keep it together anymore. There was a time when guys were proud to bring me home to meet their parents. The last time, though, I could read the disapproval and disappointment on their faces. I was skanky. My hands shook, my skin was pasty, and I was scared all the time. I couldn't remember things or predict where I'd end up each night or what would happen. I'd tell myself every day that I'd stay in, I wasn't going to go out drinking, and I'd be good. But by sundown, I was pacing, irritable, restless, lonely, feeling like I would jump out of my skin. I had to get out. I'd fire up a bowl or do a line and get ready to go out. Forgetting everything I'd promised myself just hours before, I was hell-bent on getting out. Go somewhere. Away from me.

The DC area always went through a dry drug spell each September. Broken and without a guide, I ventured further and further east of the Capitol and followed the path of lost suburban girls who did what they did to make the pain go away. In shadowed doorways and parking lots, with slow-moving, stumbling addicts, I sought any opportunity to find solace and disappear into numbness. And it didn't matter who took me there or what they wanted to do to me. I floated away, outside of my body, outside of myself, and observed my life like it was someone else's.

Undated Photo, Location Unknown

And every night, I'd find myself returning to Poseurs because I had no place else to go. Dancing, drinking, drugging, sleeping on the floor of the empty apartment above the club. Waking at 6 a.m., noshing on a bag of sliders at the counter of the Little Tavern, a twenty-four-hour burger joint, chatting with the street people, wandering DC until the club reopened at nine, roaming in and out of day bars and clothing stores, sitting in parks, and killing time.

Thomas had left me countless times to visit his other girlfriend, and here I was, a new record for me, a five-day bender.

"I can't help myself, baby. I love you both. You know it's kind of a take it or leave it thing, my love, but I know you'll take it because you love me too," he'd say, stroking my hair.

He was right. He knew I wouldn't leave him. He was exotic, a tall Chinese American boy-man with deep-green almond eyes and a wicked grin. He was fun, the sex was outrageous, and my hunger for him was constant. Most importantly, he was generous, giving me a rock of coke each morning about the size of my palm. Despite his cheating that cut my heart so deeply, enraging me, spinning me into a revenge-seeking wounded girl, I knew deep down I wouldn't break up with him. I couldn't. All I could do was drink, dance, and drug until I no longer cared. Partying full circle until I felt sober and drinking more as I waited for him to come back to me.

Time passed. I don't know how much. Then, *oh, damn,* I thought. *Work!* I jumped in the shower and quickly dressed. Taking a cab to the metro, I paused outside the building entrance back on Fifteenth Street and examined myself in a store window. *Not terrible*, I thought. And I should be close to being on time. Opening the ad agency suite entrance, the receptionist once again stared at me harshly. Getting to my seat, I saw the empty desk. Confused, I looked around in time to see Pauline striding toward me, a blend of concern and irritation on her face.

"What are you doing here, Karen?" she asked, getting straight to the point.

"Hi! Good morning. I just got here and don't know where my things are. Can you help me? Did my desk get moved?"

"Karen, we fired you last week. Do you remember? You have to leave. You don't have a job here anymore."

Everything inside me crashed, crashed down around me. Completely confused between what I remembered and what I thought I dreamed, I racked my memory, scanning the last few days. So many blank areas, like potholes in a road. Cheeks burning, shame pulling me into a quagmire of quicksand, I looked down and quickly grabbed my purse and coat.

"I'm so sorry. I must have misunderstood."

I walked to the exit, feeling every judgment and stare

slicing the back of my body.

Later that night, in early September, the wind getting colder by the minute, I left the club to drive home with Little Boy, whose actual name I'll never remember. Fumbling to find a mellow station on the radio to match my melancholy mood, my fingers flipped between the radio knob and the smooth head of the gearshift lever. I settled on a classical music station, which I never listened to, but it seemed calming, especially after spending the night immersed in the club's pounding bass. I'd known Little Boy for a year; he was young, gay, gorgeous, and happy, or so he seemed.

He shook his head as if to clear something and asked, "Why don't you leave that shit of a boyfriend? You deserve so much better, girl!"

His question hit hard. I didn't know anyone could see how blatantly my cheating shit of a boyfriend disrespected me. A cold jolt went through me when I realized how little he loved me. Just in front of me, an S-curve exit to the interstate appeared. Without a thought, I decisively floored the car, saw the speedometer shoot up to a speed I'd never driven at, and swung the steering wheel hard left with everything I had. I shut my eyes. The car skidded sideways across the exit and hit the guardrail, flipped, flipped again, and slid on its side. There was rust and metallic screeching until it came to a stop, laying mortally wounded between the two right lanes of the highway. The tenth car I had totaled.

I opened my eyes and thought, *Fuck. I can't get out of here.* Climbing out of the car, the boy and I ran down the embankment to Bob & Edith's Diner, and I called the wreck into a friend who owned a towing company. Walking back to the scene, Little Boy thanked me for the ride.

"I'm okay," he said. "Just hurt my wrist, which will get me out of work for a week!"

Nothing gets him down, I thought.

By the time we returned, another car had stopped on the shoulder. A couple got out and walked toward us.

"Are you all okay?" the woman asked.

"Fine," we replied.

The man shook his head. "Look. We saw the whole thing and called the cops. We didn't know how badly you might have been hurt. We just left DC, we saw you crash, and we'll say anything you want us to when the cops get here."

"Wow. That's really nice of you," I said as blue lights approached from behind and parked.

"Who's the driver of the car?" the officer asked.

"Any injuries? What happened? License and registration," he ordered.

"No, no one's hurt. I saw an animal shoot out from the side of the road and swerved to miss it and lost control. I left my purse at home, so I don't have my information on me," I explained as politely as I could.

The officer leaned in close to me.

"You've been drinking," he said.

"Well, yeah, I had a beer."

"You've had more than that." Turning to his partner, who was examining the wreckage, he said, "Call for a tow."

"Oh, you don't need to do that. I have a tow truck on the way."

"What? How did you call for a tow truck?"

"Well, we walked down to Bob & Edith's and used the pay phone to call my friend. He has a tow truck—"

"You left the scene of the accident," he said, brows furrowed, more menacing now. I knew why he was mad. He wouldn't be able to administer an alcohol test or charge me with anything because I had left the scene of the accident.

"I know this is a drunk driving accident," he said, his voice measured. You could hear the frustration as an undertone, though. "Because you left the scene, I can't test or charge you. Why did you leave the accident?"

"Well, officer, the car's in the middle of the highway, and I wanted to get it moved as quickly as possible so no one else would run into it," I said, wide-eyed and innocently.

But he wasn't buying it. No one was. Little Boy's eyes glistened with excited delight as he listened to the deftness by which I avoided arrest. But everyone knew I was loaded.

What no one knew was why I turned that wheel and why I couldn't seem to get out of this life.

In my dream, everything melted into shades of green: apple, sage, celery, fern, juniper, deep-emerald-jewel toned. I sat on that low rocking swing bench, suspended by a metallic green chain. I slowly lifted my head and saw the grass continue as far as I could see to my left under a dreamy green sky. My eyes followed the dense forest arching from left to right, gently encasing the velvet lawn. As the breeze swayed in the trees in slow motion, the Irish moss-covered stones dividing the immense lawn trembled and shook without a sound. Silently, the lawn split down the middle, stones falling in, ground opening in slow motion, in a direct line toward me. Shades of emerald filled my eyes, and my mind searched for any noise. No sound. Like a slow-moving river of green lava, the earth opened, releasing the ground, the stones, and the little green insects that feed off the grass, and then the porch steps disappeared into the green, steamy, ripped earth.

Waking up, I couldn't shake the feeling that I was falling. I moved to the living room floor, eyeing a foggy, dreary sunrise through the sliding deck doors. Even the sun looked half-assed. Despair and desperation seeped in, an unwanted appearance. It's like this every single day.

The phone rang. Reaching up, I picked up the receiver in a daze. *It's Mom. Jesus, just what I need.*

"What's going on, Karen? I was going to leave you a message. Why aren't you at work?"

"I got in a car accident last night, Mom. I'm okay, but I think the car is totaled."

Silence.

"That wasn't an accident, was it?"

Silence.

The line went dead.

I sat, incredulous that she knew the truth of what I had done the night before. She knew that it wasn't a simple accident but that I had intended to kill myself. Shit, I was just looking for a way out that seemed reasonable. How did she know? She always knew the truth about me, deep, deep inside of me, without me saying a word. It's like she was inside my head, always, and not in a way that felt good or protective. No, it was her cold harshness that stayed inside of me, kept me from enjoying anything, kept me second-guessing myself, always. Kept me in a low-grade state of terror, every waking moment.

When she hung up on me, she knew that I knew she saw me. And she was walking away from me for good.

Although I'd never had her or had a relationship with her that felt kind and supportive, I knew all chances of that ever happening were gone forever. And with that phone call, I'd lost any hope of further contact with my family. I was ousted, out, too sick, too bad, too dangerous. I was truly on this earth alone, and I couldn't stay in it, and I couldn't get out.

I bent over onto all fours, and my forehead dropped to the floor. "Oh, God," I groaned out loud. "I can't handle this anymore." I didn't know I'd uttered a prayer that opened a channel to universal intervention and that I'd just surrendered everything.

Universal Intervention

Vanessa Starling ran an exclusive talent recruiting agency in DC. Thomas's sister knew her vaguely, but enough that I could leverage that connection to schedule a meeting with her. Newly fired and knowing it was likely the last chance I had to get a job, I nervously entered the building on Pennsylvania Avenue and ascended to her office on the top floor. Plain gray wall-to-wall carpeting ran down the white-walled corridor lit with standard fluorescents. A faint hint of pine-scented cleaner lingered in the air. *Surprisingly nondescript for being next to the Blair House,* I thought, known as the President's Guest House for visiting dignitaries and heads of state.

I opened the door, and my senses exploded. Wild tie-dyed tapestries hung everywhere, bordered by long strands of glass beads in every shape and color. The entire waiting room ceiling was covered with fabric—blues, fuchsia, greens, golds. Incense burned in the far corner, drawing my attention to an altar with a mix of idols: Ganesha, the Hindu elephant god, sat next to a round-bellied laughing Buddha, who was cheering up a despondent-looking Virgin Mary. Disoriented, I thought I'd entered the wrong suite and turned toward the door.

"Karen! Come here," a voice commanded. Hesitantly, I stepped further into the suite, through the reception area, into a large corner office painted a soothing mauve. Two mid-century modern swivel chairs faced what looked like a hand-carved desk with inlaid mosaic tiles on the top. Behind it, smiling broadly, sat a redheaded woman with a chic modern haircut in a tie-dyed silk top. Vanessa offered her hand to shake.

"You found me. Good. Sit. What is your astrological sign?"

"My astrological sign?" I stammered, completely thrown.

"Yes. You look like fire. Are you fire," she said more as a statement than a question.

"Uh, yes. Aries," I replied, now completely unsure of what was happening. I scrambled in my bag for my résumé.

"Résumé? I don't need that. No. You know, of course, that I run the most exclusive talent agency in the city. This is the nation's capital, of course, so most of my clients are the most discerning and important clients one could have. They are important people doing important work. They pay for my services; you do not. Do you understand?"

"Yes, I do."

"I only place people based on their astrological signs, and I have had complete success in doing so. Now, how are your typing skills?"

"Fine. Do you want me to take a typing test?"

"No. Aries don't lie. If you think your typing is fine, then I'm sure it is. How is your phone presence? Do you give good information over the phone? How do you handle pressure? Do you respond quickly?"

"Well, I have a lot of experience managing high-pressure situations, especially over the phone, so I think I'm pretty good at that. Plus, I hate it when things get delayed, and I know how hard that is for customers, so I'm really quick to respond."

"Good. This is very good. I am setting you up with the National Academy of Sciences. Their HR department is full of Pisces—a total disaster. There are two spots open. The first is with a man named Chris Laughlin. He runs the recruiting effort for the academic team. It is prestigious to be recruited for the Academy. So, you need to convey that over the phone without being stuffy or off-putting. You can do that, no? I don't know exactly what Chris needs you to do, only that he needs help. He's very chatty, so when you meet him, get him talking. He'll love you for that."

She continued, "The second spot is with Caroline Corner—don't laugh, that's her actual name. She is a methodical interviewer. She will review all your information and find an angle that interests her to learn more. She will want to know how organized you are. You are organized, yes?"

I nodded.

"Good. She runs the records department, so order and organization are most important to her. She wants everything to be accounted for—on time and in an organized manner. Information needs to be easily found too."

"I like organizing things. And I like helping people. So, either spot would be great."

"You need to dress the part. Do you have something more conservative? Think about that. You need a dark suit. Do you have a dark suit? Can you get one by tomorrow?"

"I think so."

"No, you cannot think about it. You must know. It's important to look the part. Can you do that?"

"Yes."

"Good. Exactly. When you talk to each director, be yourself. Be energetic. But be serious! You will be fabulous because you are an Aries, and they will sense that energy. It is most important that I put an Aries in there to shake things up and get things done. You do get things done, yes?"

Yes. I do. Like my mother and my father, in spite of

everything, I do get things done.

In my dream, I stood on an expansive floor of an enormous clock. It stood countless stories high, with an opening in the middle of each floor, filled with large, titanic gears of every shape and size. I was alone, and everything was still. I saw my arm reach far out over the edge of the walkway I stood on, and my hand wrapped around the grip of a long handle close to me. My shoulder rotated, and I began to push the handle forward. A low rumble vibrated through the air, and the gears engaged, turning slowly, one kicking off movement in the next until they were all turning slowly. *Change is here*, a high-pitched voice crackled over a speaker, and then I awoke.

While the Academy's flagship building was prominently located on Constitution Avenue and notably registered on the National Register for Historic Places, the administrative offices were in a newer government building on Pennsylvania Avenue, not far from Vanessa's office. I arrived there early, dressed in a conservative navy pinstripe skirt suit. Thankfully, I had found it on sale at The Salvation Army thrift store with a plain white button-up blouse that was a little too big, and I was hopeful that the suit jacket would mask the poor fit. It was a chilly fall morning. I walked faster than my typical pace to warm myself since I didn't have a coat; I figured that would also help put a little color on my pale skin.

After registering as a visitor in the log at the guard desk, I rode the elevator to the seventh floor. Nervous, the pressure of my survival on the line, I entered the HR department. To my left, a short man with tousled brown hair stood from his desk and walked over to me, hand outstretched.

"You must be Karen," his warm voice greeted me. "I'm Chris. We'll talk for a bit, and then I'll walk you to your next interview."

Chris and I walked to a conference room, and he shut the door.

"You have nice legs," he casually remarked as I settled into a chair and crossed my ankles. He sat down next to me. "So, you and I would be working closely together. I'll need someone who's confident and can run things smoothly. I have a tight schedule"—he paused and smiled broadly, his crystal-blue eyes twinkling—"but I like a woman who takes charge, so I'll let you handle my calendar."

"That sounds fine!" I answered, trying to sound enthusiastic and warm but not flirty.

"Good, good. We'll have a close working relationship. You know, I've worked with a lot of young women before, but you seem the most experienced and professional, from what I can tell. I haven't been in DC for too long, just a couple of years, but from where I'm from in Pennsylvania, things are more relaxed."

"My mom is from Pennsylvania! What area are you from?"

"I could tell you had that Pennsylvanian influence! Pittsburgh. I lived there until I moved here for this job. Good beer there. There will be times when I'll need you to come with me to an evening event—you know, schmoozing with the academics. We will occasionally have late working nights too, you know, but that would also come with dinners." His warmth flushed over me, and I felt giddy, but I managed to pull out a shy smile and answered affirmatively.

Chris talked for the next twenty minutes, sharing stories of his successes with recruiting highly coveted scientific academics from a variety of disciplines. With each story, he leaned in closer until I could clearly smell his scent, a spicy blend of aftershave and desire. As discreetly as I could at such proximity, I leaned back and smiled, encouraging him to continue.

"You've enticed me to tell you everything about me!" He shifted and stood up. "I can't wait to learn more about you. I'm sure we'll be talking again very soon."

I gathered my purse, unwound my legs that had been tightly held in a stylized formation, and stood, turning slightly toward the door. Chris put his hand on my lower back and steered me, continuing his encouraging chat.

"You should hear back from Vanessa this afternoon. I think you're the most qualified for the position, and I am looking forward to working with you."

"Thank you so much for your time, Chris. I loved hearing your stories and look forward to the opportunity!"

He walked me to the opposite side of the office suite, pointed to a row of chairs next to a bank of filing cabinets, and offered me a seat. "Just wait here for a few minutes while I tell your next interviewer you're ready. But I'll let her know that I have first dibs on you!" He winked, then disappeared behind a heavy wooden office door directly ahead of me.

After what seemed like a rude amount of time to be waiting, the door opened, and Chris came out, followed by a very tall, thin, aloof-appearing woman. Her lack of warmth was immediately apparent and contrasted clearly with the energy Chris exuded. He seemed oblivious to her cold countenance.

"Thank you, Chris," Caroline said as she eyed me carefully. "Good morning. Please follow me," she said blandly, as if she had done this 400 times that morning.

We walked to the far end of the office suite, and I sat down in front of her desk.

"Please tell me what you are looking for," Caroline said, more of a slight question.

Instinctively, I toned down the enthusiasm I'd put on display for Chris. Attempting to match Caroline's more formal demeanor, I quietly talked about how I wanted to help her organize information, as I had understood that was the primary need of the job. She listened carefully without giving away any reaction or hint of understanding. No response. I could not read anything in her expression or tell whether I was connecting with her or not. She simply gave me her full attention and listened. And the more she listened, the more uncomfortable I became. I had been used to selling myself, but in this interview, my attempts to "sell," to create an emotional response, share a bit of humor, a moment of connection, fell short.

I ran out of things to say.

Panic knocked on my throat. *What do I do? What do I do now?* My thoughts spiraled.

"Is there anything else you could tell me about the job?" I suddenly asked.

Whew. Get her talking and get me out of this moment, I thought.

"Punctuality is necessary in this office," Caroline mused. "There are other people here who rely on the person in this position to answer the phones promptly. Besides a desire and an ability to organize information quickly and in a logical manner, punctuality and reliability are the other important attributes."

A cold jolt went through me. I had been fired from every job I'd had in the past two years for being late. There's no way I could get myself up on time every single day.

"I pride myself on my punctuality." The words flew out of my mouth before I even knew what was happening.

"That is good to hear," Caroline replied, the same cool expression shaping her mouth into a thin line. "I think we've covered everything. Thank you for coming in. Vanessa will call you with our decision."

Thank God, I thought. Relief melted my shoulders. This horrible interview was over, and I could leave.

Walking slowly back to the metro, I went over both interviews in my mind. I knew without a shadow of a doubt that I nailed the first interview with Chris and that I'd get an offer from him. The second one, though. *Holy crap.* I shook my head. There was just no way I connected with that woman. At least it was over, and I felt confident that I would have at least one offer from the Academy.

Arriving back at my apartment, I called Vanessa.

"How did it go?" she asked.

"Well, I think it went really well with Chris! I would love to have a chance to work for him," I replied.

"What happened with Caroline?"

"Well, I'm not sure." I hesitated. "She was hard to read. I think I answered her questions well, but I'm just not sure how I did."

"Don't worry. I'll call them both today and let you know what they thought," Vanessa promised.

Two days later, Vanessa called.

"You did wonderfully, as, of course, I knew you would," she said matter-of-factly. "Well done. Both Chris and Caroline want to hire you. After talking it through more thoroughly, Caroline insisted you are the best candidate for her position, and Chris conceded. Congratulations. You start on Monday."

A huge wave of relief mixed with startled confusion flooded me, leaving me speechless. I couldn't imagine how I'd been hired after that second interview, which felt so flat.

"Th-thank you," I managed to stammer. "You won't be

disappointed."

"I'm certain I won't," Vanessa replied. "The stars are never wrong."

"The stars are never wrong," I repeated to myself as I hung up the phone. Little did I know how the stars were aligning to shift my future. That Monday, I hustled to get to my desk on time. Six weeks later, Chris would be fired for drinking on the job. And without even knowing, my life was catapulting in an entirely new direction.

You know, the one person I needed by my side to celebrate my new kick-ass job was gone. Oh, yeah. Thomas was back in New York seeing his other boo, Jane. *It doesn't matter*, I told myself. *I don't really care. I'll grab Sam, and we'll get some boys together, and I'll celebrate my new job just fine without that asshole.*

I pulled together my favorite outfit—a black 1950s satin prom dress, rhinestone earrings that dangled to my shoulders, a rhinestone-studded black velvet choker, elbow-length black lace gloves, black fishnet stockings over fuchsia tights, and, of course, a staple in every eighties' girl's closet: Dr. Marten's 1460 boots.

Singing along to Kate Bush's *Running Up The Hill*, I poured myself a rum and Coke and lit up a bowl.

Feeling feisty and festive, out the door I skipped, bracelets jingling down the hall. I hopped in the sporty red Audi 2000 Thomas had bought me, shifted the car gleefully down the George Washington Parkway, and zipped around slower tourists, up and over the Key Bridge into Georgetown.

Exorcist Stairs, Georgetown

Parking under the Exorcist Steps, I strode confidently toward Poseurs just in time to see Sam's blond locks disappear in the doorway. *She's here*, I smiled. *By the time I get inside, she'll already have yummy drinks at the table.*

Through the dark, a glint of copper caught my eye. Pushing forward through the crowd, I saw a white T-shirt, a studded black belt around ripped black jeans, ginger hair, and a new freckled face I'd never seen before.

"Hey, Tom Sawyer!" I yelled.

He turned and smiled, green eyes locking with mine.

"Why look, it's Becky Thatcher!" His long arm reached as I continued to push toward him, and he grabbed my hand. "C'mon over here, sweet thing," he invited, still smiling wide, eyes and feet moving in a slow dance.

I wrapped my arms around this new, strange neck and hugged close, swaying with him to the music. He smelled so good, unknown, clean.

"You're new here," I said, and he nodded. "What's a nice Midwestern-lookin' farm boy like you doing here?"

"Lookin' for you," he whispered, easy in my ear. Heat

tingled up my spine.

We sat at the back table on the stage for hours under the video screen. He told stories, entertaining the table. Although I was sitting next to him, aware of his side pressed against mine, I couldn't keep up with the chatter and watched my table mates for cues of when to laugh or smile. A couple of lines of coke and many drinks later, I found myself in the passenger seat of his VW Bug. He parked in his apartment building garage and turned to look at me, brushing a strand of hair from my left cheek. "You're sweet," he murmured. "You're going to like what I've got inside."

We entered his modern, two-bedroom apartment. The calm, light, and airy space furnished with luxurious cream, white, and light gray furniture impressed me. "In here," he directed, pointing to his bedroom. I followed him to the left side suite. It was dark, masculine. "I have a surprise for you," he said as he opened the walk-in closet, revealing racks of lace lingerie, ropes, and an abundant assortment of leather straps, masks, whips, and handcuffs.

"Uh, I don't think I'm in Kansas anymore," I said hesitantly, referencing *The Wizard of Oz*.

"Put this on," he said as he handed me a combination of lace and leather.

"I don't really know how this works," I slurred, getting more confused as I turned the pieces over in my hands.

"I'll help you," he said, and then, in a colder voice, "Strip."

Confidence draining with each passing second, I undressed, confused by the confluence of clumsy seduction and embarrassment. He held out the first lace piece. "Step here. And now here."

I stood, adorned now in a lace bra and thong, leather straps running in various configurations around my body. Somewhere between comfortable and uncomfortable, feeling ridiculous and hilarious, a tiny giggle escaped my lips. He ignored my awkward silence and grew more aroused at the visual before him.

"Now lay down," he ordered, and I thankfully fell backward on the bed, pulling back the covers.

"No, turn over," he said, grabbing my ankles and flipping me over onto my stomach.

I shifted my shoulders and chest down into the thickness of the down comforter, resting my head on my hands, and closed my eyes, finally succumbing to the fogginess swirling around my head as he entered me. *I don't care*, I thought as sleep washed away the sounds and smells of the night I had chosen, avoiding the reality of going home alone once again.

Sudden pounding on the door. *BOOM, BOOM, BOOM.*

"POLICE," yelled a voice, and the front door blew open. I opened my eyes, grabbed the covers, and rolled to my left, covering myself as three police officers entered the bedroom. As my Tom Sawyer jumped up naked, two officers grabbed him and pinned him to the bed.

"Alex Taylor, you're under arrest," the first officer said, clamping handcuffs on his wrists.

The third officer looked at me, barely able to keep a smirk off his face. "Get dressed. Where's your ID?" he asked.

"Uh, do I have to give you my ID?" I asked.

"No, you're not under arrest. But do you know who this guy is?" the officer asked. "He's a bad guy. Yep, you're under arrest for assault and attempted murder, my friend," he said, turning to Alex.

They started hauling Tom/Alex out of the apartment. "Hey, how am I going to get out of here?" I shouted.

"Keys—table," Alex yelled as the police dragged him out the door.

The door shut, leaving behind a thunderous silence and

hammer in my head. Fighting a thick cotton mouth, feeling nauseous and panicked about the time, I fumbled my way through the early morning light to find my clothes. After showering quickly, I grabbed the car keys and stumbled through the apartment hallways until I found an elevator. Opening to the garage level, I realized I didn't know which car was his, only that it was a VW Bug. But what color? Where did we park? Wandering around the aisles, I tried the key in the locks of different Volkswagens until, at last, the key fit.

I drove back into Georgetown and found my car right where I'd left it. I parked Tom/Alex's car a few spaces away, slipped the keys in the cup holder, and shut the door on that terrible night. I hopped back into my happy little car and drove down M Street. *At least I'll get to work on time for once*, I thought, knowing how reliably late I usually was to work.

Parking a few blocks away at a garage with a cheaper day rate, I trotted up Pennsylvania Avenue and morphed into Daytime Karen, the one with the new job at the National Academy of Sciences. Arriving at my desk, I sat quickly and cupped my hand, breathing into it, checking my breath. I sat back and closed my eyes for a moment, gathering myself. No one else was in; I'd beat everyone into the office for once. A thin stream of bile shot up my throat, and I swallowed quickly. A wave of nausea hit me, and I doubled over with a hard cramp. Sweating, I bolted from my chair and made it just in time to the ladies' room, where everything from the night before exploded in a volcanic eruption. Heaving, wrapping my arms around the white ceramic toilet bowl, I emptied myself, then turned and emptied myself again from the other end.

Weak, sweat dripping from my armpits down my torso, pale as a translucent slice of onion, I splashed water on my face, patted my matted hair back into some semblance of a professional look, and straightened my dress. Rail thin, the skirt section floated and bounced along my jagged hip bones. I clomped my way back down the hall and reentered the office, suddenly abuzz with activity. Everyone was in, the loud office sounds of phones ringing, people chattering in low office voices, IBM Selectric typewriters clacking away.

My two office mates stared at me as I made my way back to my seat. One approached me, a careful, concerned look in her eyes. "Are you okay? We saw your purse but didn't see you for at least an hour. Don't worry. I covered your phones for you."

"Thanks. I'm fine. I haven't been gone that long. I was only in the bathroom for a few minutes."

"Oh, okay. Well, I've been here for over an hour, and you were gone when I arrived, so I was just worried. Glad you're okay." She returned to her seat, darting a glance at the receptionist.

I walked to my desk and saw a stack of files. I was behind on filing, and more than almost anything else, I hated filing. So boring, so repetitive, so insulting. I picked up a light stack of manila folders and approached the wall of six-foot filing cabinets. Bland gray drawers stared back at me. Reaching with my left hand, I opened a drawer and flipped through the army-green hanging folders until I found the location for the first folder. Sliding it into its usual home, I looked at the next folder and took three steps to my right to the next filing cabinet. Again, I opened the heavy drawer with my left hand and—

Weird. I had a weird sensation. Looking down, I noticed I was wearing different shoes. Red pumps I didn't recognize. I swung my head up and saw the bank of filing cabinets. But something was different; I had a panicky sense that something was off, and then slowly, slowly, I realized it was a different day. I'd lost time somehow, and I didn't know what day it was. Taking a sharp breath, I slowly turned and made my way back to my desk. My knees were stiff; I was trying to walk casually, but it came off wooden. I was still clutching a few folders, now slightly bent in the middle from my hard grip. I put them down and stared at the desk calendar. *I don't know what day it is*, my brain screamed as I tried to figure it out.

"Hey! Do you want to go to lunch?" my office mate asked. It's lunchtime.

"Vie de France has tarragon chicken on special today. You like that, right?" she continued.

The tarragon chicken salad special is on Tuesdays. *Tuesday tarragon. Oh god, office mate, you're an angel.*

"Uh, sure, thanks. I'll meet you there," I promised, knowing full well I wouldn't go. The stack of files had grown since I last remembered seeing them. Plus, that woman talked too much.

The days passed in a similar fashion. Most nights, I spent on the three Ds: drinking, drugging, and dancing, mostly at Poseurs because I didn't know where else to go. Each night, I'd tell myself I was going to stay in, not go downtown, not drink for once, not go to Poseurs because God, it was *so boring there*, and every night, I'd find myself back on that stage, at the same table, whiskey in my hand, Simple Minds playing in my brain. And each morning, it was the same routine: run from the Foggy Bottom metro station up the street and collapse at my desk. Check the time: 8:35. *Maybe no one will notice I'm late again.* Feel that bile rise and threaten again.

Make it just in time to the ladies' room and vomit, purge. Clean myself up and return to my desk as if nothing was wrong. Nothing to see here, folks. Just move along.

One average Wednesday morning, Caroline opened her office door. "Karen, would you come into my office?" She directed me in a kind but authoritative voice. Not really a request.

Sitting expectantly behind her desk, she looked directly at me, elegant in her gray single-breasted suit, salt-and-pepper hair styled into a classic cross bun. Although I'd only just started as her assistant, she wanted to chat about my performance.

"How do you think you are doing here?" she asked in a gentle voice.

I didn't know how to answer that. A small panic began to rise, and I felt my cheeks burn.

"The girls tell me you disappear into the bathroom as soon as you arrive in the morning," she continued. "They are covering the phones for you until you get back to your desk, which takes at least thirty minutes each day. And some have reported that they hear you vomiting in the toilet."

Oh my god. They knew. Panicking hard, my arms itching, breaking out into a cold sweat, a wave of anger hit me, and I bit my lower lip. I couldn't deny it, but I still couldn't speak. I looked at my boss, ashamed, and quickly looked away.

"I know how you may be feeling, Karen. I called you in here to talk because ten years ago, my boss reached out to me when I was struggling, and I was able to get help. I drank too much and needed help. It is now my turn to give that gift back to you. So, I would like to ask you, do you have any problems that you want to tell me about? Because if you do, I will help you. The Academy will help you. But only if you want to tell me, and that choice is yours."

I looked at my hands. Ocean waves of anger and

humiliation washed over me. I opened my mouth and haltingly said, "Yes, well. Sometimes I drink a little at night to help me go to sleep. I'm under a lot of stress."

"Okay. I understand. You are very brave, telling me the truth. I understand. If you would like us to help you, then take this number"—she held out a scrap of paper—"and call it. There is someone on the other side who is waiting for you."

Looking down at the floor, cheeks red and burning, I mumbled something, took the paper from Caroline's hand, and walked out the door. Furious and humiliated, I headed to my desk. Instead of sitting down, I walked to the right corner of my desk and, almost in disbelief, watched my hand, now operating independently of my own thought, pick up the phone and dial the number Caroline had given to me. *What am I doing?* I thought as panic again made its unwelcome entrance.

"Is this Karen?" a woman's voice asked, clear and strong.

"Yes."

"I've been expecting your call. I'm waiting for you. Come to room 718 now. It's just down the hall on the left side."

I hung up, stood for a moment, and then walked out of the office area. Opening the door, I peered down the dimly lit hallway. No one around. I exited right and counted the office suite numbers down: 722, 721, 720, 719. On the left, just as promised, was 718. I stood outside the closed door. A sign centered on the door at a man's eye level: HEALTH OFFICE. Below it was an availability indicator: *The Nurse Is In.* I opened the door and entered the sterile, empty reception area. Three closed doors surrounded the reception desk. White walls, white doors, white linoleum tile. The middle door suddenly opened, startling me. A very tall nurse filled the doorway. Also dressed in white, her stern eyes commanded all my attention.

"Karen, come in. My name is Kate Mākris. I'm the head nurse here at the Academy. I have been waiting for you. Sit down."

"Okay."

"Do you know why you are here talking to me today?"

"Well, it's like I told Caroline, sometimes I drink a little too much to relax, and—"

Kate stood, her six-foot frame looming over me.

"You are here because you are doing drugs," her voice boomed. "You are in withdrawal right now. Do you know how I can tell? You are scratching your arms!"

I froze, doe-eyed, staring back at her. I looked down and saw that, yes, I had been scratching both arms. From the looks of the long, sharp red streaks, I was doing it constantly without knowing it.

Kate's long arm shot out, finger pointing right between my eyes. "If you don't do exactly what I tell you to do, you will die! Do you realize that?"

I shuddered uncontrollably. Terrified, I thought, *How does she know?* And then a bolt blasted through my insides.

"Do you have cameras?" I whispered.

"We know everything, Karen. Now listen to me. How fast can you pack your things? The only way you will live is if you go to a treatment center. The only question is this: where do you want to go? You have three choices: Minnesota, Nebraska, or North Carolina."

It's October, I thought. *North Carolina will still be warm.*

"I'll go to North Carolina."

"Good. Is there anybody you need to tell? You will be gone for quite some time. You are very sick."

"Well, yes, my parents. But I can't tell them. You don't understand. My mom will literally kill me." I started crying. Fear poured itself over the terror I already felt.

"I will come with you. You won't be alone. I will drive you to your parent's house, and then we will go to your apartment and get you packed. Can we go tonight? Your plane will leave tomorrow, early in the morning."

"I can call my dad. I'll ask him if I can come over."

"Good. Do that. Now go home and start packing."

Dropping the Bags

That evening, I arrived with Kate at the massive brick home my parents were so proud of. I had called ahead of time and asked if I could come over. As we pulled up the driveway, I could see my parents sitting tensely in the living room from the front window.

"Welcome home, love," my father said as I entered, a cautious smile on his face, his eyes wary. "What brings us this pleasure? And who is your friend?"

I sat, trembling inside. "This is Kate, a nurse from the National Academy of Sciences, where, as you know, I work."

"Hello, Mr. and Mrs. Marginot," Kate said simply and warmly.

"Oh, please. Call us Chuck and Joanne," my mom said. "Can I offer you something to drink?"

"No, thank you," Kate replied. "I'm here with Karen to help her discuss a difficult topic. Should we sit?"

"Yes, of course," my dad said. "What do you want to tell us, love?" he asked as he sipped his drink.

"Well, I have some news," I said.

"Oh, I'm sure you want money," my mom blurted out sarcastically.

"Joanne," my father intervened, stopping her.

"Okay, I guess I'll just tell you. Well, you know I have this new job—"

"You're fired. Of course, you're fired," my mom interrupted.

"No. Not exactly. Well, as it turns out, my boss thought that I needed some help."

"You don't need help, Karen. You've had nothing *but* help from us. What you need to do is stop being so selfish and get your life together."

"Well, my boss thinks that I have a problem with alcohol. She thinks that I need to go to a treatment center and get well."

My father, clenching his Manhattan, slumped back into his leather mid-century recliner, helpless, and then stared down into his glass, looking for an answer.

"Oh really? We'd rather you just die, Karen," my mother responded coldly and stared at me, her fury unleashed, demanding that I—what? Implode on the spot? Disappear into ash in front of her eyes? How many times I'd tried that, tried to die, to leave this life steeped in pain, only to fail and fail again.

Kate intervened, "It's completely understandable that you are angry and upset. Family members are affected too when someone in their family suffers from alcoholism and addiction."

"Suffers?" My mom growled, jaw set, hard. "You have no idea. What she put us through. What she put her father through. You are an embarrassment to all of us, Karen. And the damage you've done to your sister, well—I don't know how she will ever recover. As far as I'm concerned, out of sight, out of mind. You are out of my concern, as you have been for many, many years. I washed my hands of you years ago. I—"

"Mrs. Marginot. I understand how angry you are, but this does not help Karen."

"I have helped her enough!" my mom retorted, her voice rising to a near shout.

"Joanne. Let Karen and her friend finish. Please," my dad tried redirecting her.

My mom glared at him and, with a flourish, stormed out of the living room.

Frozen inside, I stared at the tops of my shoes.

Kate continued, "Karen is here to let you know that she'll be staying at a residential treatment center in North Carolina. I am driving her to the airport tomorrow morning and will make sure she arrives safely. After the doctors assess her, they will put together a treatment plan to detail how long they recommend she stay."

"What is this going to cost us?" my mom shouted from the kitchen.

"The Academy is taking care of the cost, Mrs. Marginot," Kate assured her.

"Oh, aren't you a lucky girl," my mom sarcastically said.

"We are here tonight to let you know what is going on and so Karen can pack anything she wants to take. I will leave you information about the treatment center and the family programs, should you decide to participate." Kate looked at me and asked, "Is there anything else you wanted to let your parents know at this time, Karen?"

"No," I mumbled and got up, sprinting up the stairs to my old bedroom, stomach clenched. After a moment, Kate joined me with a small suitcase I hadn't even noticed. We quickly packed a few sentimental things and returned downstairs.

"Take good care of yourself, love," my father said, hugging me close and kissing me on the forehead. My mother was nowhere to be seen.

"Thank you, Dad," I choked out, tears welling. Turning quickly, I left, Kate following a moment later.

We drove back to my apartment in silence, for the most part. At one point, Kate reached over and patted my hand.

"That was hard, I know," she said sympathetically. "But you did it, and that part is over. I'm very proud of how you handled yourself. You can leave that behind you now and focus on yourself."

"Thank you, Kate," I said when we parked. Taking the suitcase out of the back seat, I asked, "I guess I should finish packing a few things from my apartment and just get ready to see you in the morning?"

"Yes. Plan on me picking you up at six-thirty tomorrow morning. Then you'll be on your way."

Early Friday, Kate picked me up and drove me to Washington National Airport. Sitting at the gate with me, Kate handed me the book, *Alcoholics Anonymous*, commonly referred to as the Big Book, inscribed with the message, "Today is the first day of the rest of your life."

Inscription from Kate

"What are you going to do after you get out of treatment, Karen?" she asked.

"Well, I guess I'll get back together with Thomas and go back to work," I replied, a slight edge to my voice.

"You can't get back together with that guy. If that's your intention, then I don't know why we're wasting our time with you. You have no desire to stop drinking, do you?"

"Uh, no. I mean, I can see giving up the drugs, right? But drinking? That's a hard no for me," I explained.

Kate shook her head, disgusted. "I don't know why I'm wasting my time," she repeated. "Your chances are less than zero." She looked to her right, away from my direction, a thin wrinkle line appearing above her left eye.

A deep anger burned in my stomach. *I don't know what she expects*, I thought. *I mean, I'm twenty-three. Who stops drinking at twenty-three? And less than a ZERO chance? HA! I'll show you.* The argument in my head grew more intense as we sat in silence.

The American Airlines agent made the boarding announcement, and I stood up, grabbing the handle of my carry-on bag.

"Bye, Kate," I said casually as I turned and walked toward the tunnel.

"Take care, Karen," Kate replied, suddenly sincere. That was the last time I spoke with her—and the most care I'd received from an adult woman.

Sitting down on the nearly empty American Airlines flight, I ordered a gin and tonic even though it was early in the morning. I didn't want to drink but knew deep down that was the last opportunity I would have. I ordered another, mulling over how I didn't even want to get clean. I just wanted to do whatever the Academy wanted me to do and return to my job and Thomas, who I was sure would be worried that I had disappeared. I didn't have a chance to say goodbye.

The treatment center was in Charlotte, North Carolina, too far to travel back to Northern Virginia on my own, and no one could rescue me. I'd run out of money, people, and time.

The city of Charlotte rose from its Old Southern history, predating the American Revolution. Named for King George III's wife, Queen Charlotte, the town's original design mapped to the colonial style of a simple block grid. In Charlotte, the first gold rock in North America was found, igniting the first gold rush. The railroad industry boomed, and then Charlotte became a hub of cotton mills. A love of its Confederate past could still be seen in window displays of the Stars and Bars, the familiar flag of Southern pride, evoking racism, white supremacy, and a social resentment simmering just below boiling point.

In 1985, drug rehabilitation centers were called "treatment centers." I boarded the plane for the southernmost city I'd ever traveled to without knowing what to expect; as far as I knew, I was going in for hair, nails, a short nervous breakdown, and a grudging agreement to stop doing coke. It didn't dawn on me that I would be surrounded by people raised in the Deep South. How would that affect my ability to trust and heal? All I knew was that I was tired, so bone-tired. It's the most exhausting state of being when you're trying desperately to look like you know what you are doing while you are disintegrating from the inside out. For the first time, I stopped trying and let myself dissolve into the mess I truly was. I didn't know what was coming next. I knew my life as I'd known it was over. In the spiritual realm, I could sense enormous gears slowly turning; change was upon me, and I could no longer stop it from coming.

I don't remember who picked me up from the airport or how I got to the center. I do remember walking into reception, dropping my bags, and announcing loudly that the staff could take my bags to my room. Arrogance reigned. A nurse with her hair up in a huge blond beehive, looking more like a classic diner waitress than medical staff, chuckled from behind her glass-enclosed office and said, "Honey child, you aren't at the Ritz. Do you even know where you are?"

An orderly with a body built for intimidation picked up my bags, took them to another room behind another pane of glass, and searched them. Out came my birth control pills, my Valium, and my vibrators. The sudden rage boiling up surprised even me. Out of control, my fists started banging on the glass, shouting, "YOU CAN'T TAKE THOSE. THOSE ARE MY PERSONAL THINGS. DO YOU EVEN KNOW WHO I AM? DO YOU KNOW WHO MY FATHER IS? I'M FROM WASHINGTON, DC. I WILL HAVE YOUR JOBS."

A quick sting in the thigh.

Waking up, I found myself dry-mouthed, confused, and groggy in a solo room. A sterile cot covered in plastic in the corner, a simple wooden chair. No light switch, window, or door handle. No one was around. I paced for hours. Minutes? A day? The door opened, and a burly female nurse with a deep bass voice entered.

"You ready to calm down?"

I nodded.

She motioned to me to follow her, and we walked silently down an ill-lit corridor to the women's section. She opened a door to the right, and I entered phase two—shared quarters. There were four single beds, little more than cots, placed in each corner of the room. One overhead light and my suitcase at the foot of the bed.

"The other women are in group right now," the nurse said. "Sit here and wait until they get back. Then you'll all come for lunch."

Sitting, I could not do, but pacing, I did well. And so I paced for what seemed like an hour, although it was probably no more than fifteen minutes. The door opened. My new roommates entered.

At a loss for how to approach them, I managed a low "How long have you been here?" to all and no one in particular.

Cindy was the first to answer. In her early forties, she had been a closet heroin addict, but her husband arranged an intervention before she lost her sweet Southern girl looks and all that bought.

"I'm almost done," she beamed. "I get out of here on Friday. Don't worry, sweetie, you're going to do great. I can just tell." Cindy offered sunshine, hope, and encouragement. I was betting she found her calling as a cheerleader in high school and never let it go.

Pat was dark, brooding, edgy. "I got here last week," she said simply, then curled up on her bed, turning away from everyone.

Kathy didn't answer but walked to the window and looked out, elbow on the windowsill, lost in her thoughts.

They brought Twelve Step meetings to us. They told us it would take five full years of abstinence before we would truly be sober. *Fuck that. FIVE YEARS until I would actually be sober?* I knew I was ready to give up cocaine and all the pills (I mean, you could go to jail for those), but sweet Jesus, I didn't think they were completely serious about the alcohol.

We were thoroughly scheduled with a variety of activities, including physical exams, Twelve Step meetings inside the center and out in the community, individual therapy, and group therapy. We also read, studied recovery literature, and wrote a lot. We ate three full meals a day, took showers every day, and carefully orchestrated sleep and wake times.

They scheduled us to go on daily walks around a pond, where I fell in love with a guitar-picking, bluegrass-playing yodeler from South Carolina. He said he believed in me. My counselor, Charles, said that he believed in me. He explained how addiction worked, that it was like a light switch; once turned on, I couldn't turn it off. We discovered that my drug of choice was alcohol; it's what I started with at eleven and what cost me nearly everything at twenty-three.

In treatment, October 1985

"So how did you get here?" Charles asked, scanning the sunny living room. It was a room full of Southern charm: an old piano in the far-left corner, a bank of floor-to-ceiling windows overlooking a soft green lawn, a gentle pond with benches strategically placed to take in the landscape. Tulip magnolia, ginkgo, and magnolia trees offered early fall color.

"Uh, I drove here," Randy answered. A few chuckles and giggles snuck out.

"Let's go around the room. Start by introducing yourself and telling us a little bit about how you got here," Charles responded gently.

He seems nice, I thought. I could sense a calm way about him. But there was a gentle firmness too; he seemed at ease corralling the group into focus.

One by one, the twelve newest residents introduced themselves, some haltingly, some defiantly, and some seemingly defeated. When it was her turn to share, Kathy, my new roommate, jumped in, surprisingly perky.

"Y'all knows my kin Tom. He uppin left here's afore he got released. You knows him Charles, right? And he done kilt hisself in a truck wreck last week, and I's all a-cryin and such. My moms makin all kins of a ruckus, and she tole me I gots to git clean and stay, not like Tom but stay fer the whole thang."

"Okay, Kathy, thank you for sharing that. I'm sorry about your cousin Tom. He was a good man; I do remember him. And what town does your family come from?" Charles asked.

"High Point. Best tootin' hometown in all o' Carolina!"

"High Point? HIGH POINT?" I shouted, jumping up. "That's the worst shit-town I've ever been in! There's nothing but idiot ignorant fucking rednecks there!"

Kathy jumped to her feet, eyes blazing, hot, fists clenched tight. I grabbed the metal folding chair next to me and, in one swing, threw it at her as she took a step toward me.

I was tackled to the ground. Another quick sting in my thigh, and everything went black.

Waking up, I found myself back in that small square white room—in isolation. A simple cot with the familiar plastic covering in the corner, but this time, no chair since, apparently, I turned chairs into weapons. I sat for hours; then the door opened, and that same burly female nurse with the deep bass voice entered.

"You ready to calm down?"

I nodded.

"It's time for dinner. Come on."

Accompanied by my now familiar nurse escort, I joined the line outside the cafeteria a few minutes before the doors opened.

"You're going to be good, right?" my escort asked me, more making a point than asking a question.

"Yes," I responded, realizing just how tired I was of fighting everything.

"Okay. Enjoy your dinner," she said as she turned back down the hall to her regular work.

A few bodies ahead of me stood Kathy, waiting with the rest of the line to enter the cafeteria. Not sure if I should try to talk to her, I decided to wait until we sat inside and ate dinner. *Maybe I can grab a seat next to her and apologize*, I thought. *I mean, I don't know what came over me. I've never done anything like that before.*

Moving with the line like a small train inching through a mountain pass, I finally received the evening's offering, loaded my tray, and turned, scanning the room for Kathy. She sat alone near the wall of windows.

"Hi. Please don't freak out. I just want to talk to you. Is it okay if I sit here?" I asked.

"Sure. I don't care." Kathy stared out the window.

Placing my tray down, I said, "Listen. I don't know what happened to me. I don't normally act like that. But I'm sorry I freaked out on you. I'm sure you're probably nice and everything. It didn't have anything to do with you. I just have really bad memories of that town"—I sucked my breath in sharply—"and I guess when you said it was great, it just kind of blew my mind. But really, I shouldn't have freaked out, and I'm sorry for the way I acted."

There it was—awareness of the impact of my behavior. An apology. Without me even knowing it, the Twelve Steps were beginning to weave their way into my consciousness. It was the start of step ten: continue to take personal inventory, and when we are wrong, promptly admit it. Normally, I would have focused on what a crap person she was, what a crap town she came from, and all the ways I'd been harmed there. But for some reason, what was more important to me at that moment was apologizing for how I was out of line. I knew I would keep running into her throughout my stay and just wanted things to be okay between us.

Days moved by in a blur. I met with doctors, psychiatrists, nutritionists. I was told I weighed in at eighty-five pounds and would not be released until I gained a minimum of fifteen pounds. My wrist bones scared me, as did my collarbones that stuck out so visibly. I hadn't looked at myself in years or noticed how much of my body had simply disappeared.

The harder internal work began in sessions with my counselor, Charles. During my first individual session, he explained that he was a recovering addict, over five years clean.

"When did you first use drugs or alcohol? This is where we'll begin," he asked, leaning back in his office chair.

On Saturdays, in that space between childhood and womanhood, the summer before I entered my teens, my friend Linda and I walked down to the woods. Linda was a year older than me. Taller, with a model's physique honed from years of gymnastics, Linda was everything I wanted to be: olive-skinned, with deep-green eyes, long light brown hair, and an easy laugh. She seemed to move through life with ease, confident but not cocky, with a breezy attitude and a ready laugh always on hand.

We spent as much time as we could in the woods behind my house, chasing small minnows in the stream and capturing tadpoles. We sat with our backs against the tall maples and oaks until the sun lowered toward dusk, talking for hours about boys, parents, and dreams, smoking cigarettes stolen from our mothers' purses.

One early Saturday in October, the sound of hammering drew us into the woods faster. The sound grew louder, and we looked up into the treetops. Two men were high up in adjacent trees; a third was below, passing up wooden slats for the other two to pound into the trunks.

"You're a little old for treehouses, don't you think?" I yelled. The man on the ground turned and stared at us.

Tom was the first one down from the tree. Older, with long, messy brown hair and wide eyes, his quick grin sent warm goosebumps up my arms. The younger, tall, blond man named Carl put down the board he held and waved to the last man in the tree, motioning him to climb down. Frank slid his way down the fifteen-foot drop from the branch he straddled and landed softly on the leaf-covered ground.

They walked over to us and sat down on the streambed.

"We're traveling through," Tom explained, "making a little shelter for the night."

Frank threw his head back and laughed, open-mouthed and loud. "That's one way of putting it," he quipped.

Linda glanced at me, a question mark in her eyes.

"What do you mean?" I asked.

"Oh, we're on our way north and just setting up camp for a night or two," Tom casually explained. "You girls from around here?"

"Oh yeah," I said, pointing behind me toward the right. "I'm just up the hill there. See that house with the big deck?

That's mine, and Linda lives across the street in my old house."

"What do you mean, your old house?" Frank asked.

"Well, we used to live where Linda lives, and then we moved across the street. Linda's family moved in about a year ago."

"I never heard of that, moving across the street," Tom said.

"Yeah, it was fun actually! We had a party, and everybody came over and carried our stuff to our new house."

"Well, isn't that nice," Carl said quietly.

There was a long pause. And then we told them about our lives, our families, looking for ways to showcase how sophisticated our thinking was. Carl, the quietest of the three, offered us another cigarette. Tom casually pulled one from the pack, put it softly between his lips, flicked on a lighter, and inhaled, lighting the cigarette. Holding it between his thumb and index finger, he offered the first one to me and then repeated the process for Linda.

"You've got to be hungry," I said, and Linda nodded, sizing up Carl, the youngest, and running her hands through her hair. "You want to come to my house and get some lunch?" I said.

"Oh no, ma'am," Tom said, smiling.

Linda pulled me aside and whispered, "Let's go make them some lunch."

"We'll be right back!" I said with tempered excitement. We walked quickly up the hill to my back door and ran to my room.

"They are so hot!" Linda squealed.

"I have to change. My clothes look stupid. I hate this shirt," I said, throwing open the doors to my closet.

"Do you have that red shirt I can borrow?" Linda asked. I nodded and tossed it to her.

Rummaging the closet, I quickly found what I was looking

for: an olive and brown paisley halter top I had made in Home Economics and a pair of gold bell-bottom hip-hugger jeans. Sliding into those tight jeans gave me the confidence boost I hoped for. Feeling ready, we packed up three PB&Js, poured lemonades, and carefully trotted back down my backyard, slowing to a catwalk as smoothly as our pre-teen bodies could manage when the men were within sight, holding out our offerings. The men finished their lunches quietly, humoring our questions:

"So, where are you from exactly?"

"Down south."

"And where exactly are you going?"

"Up north."

Carl shifted and sighed. Tom thanked us for the lunch and told us we were nice girls. Frank stood and, leaning back on one leg, studied us.

"Y'all shouldn't be talking to us anymore. You need to get on home now."

We hesitated, wanting to stay.

"Thanks again," Carl said as he stood and turned away.

Tom smiled a wide, wicked grin, his eyes twinkling. "The boys said it's time for you to go, so git." He joined the others, walking back to where they'd left their wood planks, and hoisted himself up to his position in the tree. We waited a moment longer, watching, but it was as if they didn't see us at all and had never seen us there. A giddy confusion swirled softly in my chest. It was as if we'd opened a door, seen something new inside, and shut it. All I knew was that Tom smelled good, and when he flashed his smile, my knees nearly buckled under me.

"Let's go," I said to Linda, and we returned to our homes, a different world a quarter of an acre away.

The news broke as we walked to school the next morning. It had rained last night, and those men we'd spent the afternoon with were captured in a house that wasn't mine.

"Did you hear the sirens last night? Did you hear the gunshots?" Linda asked me. "My mom said they broke into the house behind yours and hid in the attic. There was a shoot-out! At least one of the guys was shot to death by the police. They had escaped from Lorton prison! One was a murderer! I don't know which one, though."

My heart nearly stopped. My breath caught in my throat, and I stood still on the sidewalk, mind racing to take it all in.

"They were really nice! I can't believe this. They could have hurt us, Linda. No one knew we were talking to them. They didn't, though. They didn't hurt us or do anything to us. They weren't bad guys."

We arrived at school, and my body swirled with the collision of too many worlds careening at once. I walked from class to class, hearing nothing but a resounding protest in my mind: *they weren't bad guys*. Nothing made sense to me, and nothing else could penetrate my head.

Later that evening, as with so many weeknights, Linda and I stayed at her house, babysitting our siblings while our parents fixed dinner and played bridge at my house. Still upset and confused about what had happened to the men we met in the woods, I sat in the large basement rec room while Linda got her brother and my sister set up with a game. Linda's father had traveled the world extensively for work, with their most recent assignment (prior to moving to my old home) in Mexico. They had artifacts from their travels all around their home. Looking up, I noticed for the first time that a thin white shelf lined the perimeter of the room, up high near the ceiling. And it was full of tequila bottles. They looked beautiful, like hand-blown works of art. Most of the bottles were clear, with bright labels. Some had what looked like multicolored, intricate crystal toppers, like perfume bottles. I stared at them intently, especially at the seals around the tops. They all looked brand-new and unopened.

"Go play your game upstairs, guys," I said to our siblings. My sister looked up.

"Okay! C'mon, let's go upstairs," she cheerfully agreed, grabbing Linda's brother's hand as they trotted together.

I looked at Linda.

"You know, if we took a sip out of every one of those bottles, the levels would stay the same, and no one would notice they'd been opened. But we would have to drink the same amount out of every bottle—one sip each."

"You're right!" Linda exclaimed. Feeling a little giddy, I stood on the side arm of the couch and reached up, pulling down bottle #1.

"For-ta-LE-za," I read.

Linda giggled. "Your Spanish is horrible."

I twisted the seal around the top, and it broke. I carefully pulled off the artful glass stopper and smelled the tequila. A slight spicy citrus scent hinted behind the strong alcohol. Holding the bottle by the neck, I tilted it back, took one large swig, and passed it to Linda. The immediacy of the drink hit the back of my throat, and a bolt of energy danced down my limbs. Emboldened, I climbed back up to the shelf and pulled down the next bottle to the right. Wordless, I repeated the same process: remove top, tilt, swig, and pass. We drank, mostly in silence, eyes sparkling and getting more slit as we made our way around the room. The drinks tasted simultaneously all the same and slightly different. As each swallow went down, I felt better and better, warm inside.

My confidence grew; I suddenly felt self-assured in a way I'd always wanted but never known. I felt increasingly calm, happy, courageous, and quietly excited. I felt like myself, like I should always feel. This is what I'd been looking for my entire life.

It felt as though time stopped for us. It didn't matter anymore whether we got caught or how long it took us to travel through Mexico in Linda's basement. All that mattered was that we finished drinking the same amount from each bottle.

The phone rang, and I picked it up.

"Karen?" My mother. Ugh. "It's time for dinner. Bring everyone over to our house."

I giggled. "You're late! You're late! For a very important date!" I sang out, quoting the White Rabbit, and fell back on the couch, bursting into peals of laughter.

"I'm so drunk!" Linda shouted, and our hysterical laughter peaked.

Catching my breath, I sat up. "Okay," I said. "Let's get the kids and go over."

"They're going to know," Linda said, suddenly fearful. "They're going to know we're drunk."

I thought for a moment and found an emboldened, new, fearless me inside.

"No, they won't. They're drunk themselves! Plus, they don't care. They care more about who's winning in bridge than anything else. They just want us to eat and come back over here so they can finish their game. It'll be fine."

Confidence landed squarely in every part of my being. I suddenly felt two inches taller. My stride seemed longer; I felt stronger physically, mentally, and emotionally. The fear that was normally part of my every thought, every decision, had simply vanished. I could see everything with a new clarity. Things came sharply into focus, and all my former meek hesitation was gone. I felt truly, fully, alive.

Age 11

Fueled by this newfound strength, I took charge, even though Linda was older than me and I normally followed her lead.

"Let's go!" I firmly stated and grabbed her hand, pulling her up from the couch.

"I'm a little dizzy," Linda complained, worried.

"Don't worry; it'll pass. You just need to get outside. Take a deep breath of fresh air, and you'll be fine."

It was as if I knew exactly what to do and what to say. Suddenly patient with my sister, a rush of love flooded over me for her, and I felt protective in a way I'd never experienced.

"C'mon, let's go get dinner," I said, holding my hand to her.

We walked catty-corner across the street into my house. A warm, earthy scent of beef, freshly roasted, flooded my senses.

"Girls, set the table," my mom called to me and Linda. We moved around the table, occasionally bumping into each other, breaking out in more giggles.

"Those girls could set a giggle record." My dad smiled as he came into the dining room.

We sat and ate. Everything tasted incredibly good. Linda and I shared glances periodically as our parents chatted throughout dinner. Our siblings ate fast so they could return to their games. The smell of wine from my father's glass, just outside my plate, wafted into my head, and suddenly, that was all I was aware of. Dinner was pleasant and full of ease, but my mind was on that wine.

"Can I have a sip of your wine, Dad?" I asked as innocently as I could.

My dad's eyebrow arched. "Maybe in a few years, honey," he said as he looked at me intently. He smiled, but I could see a question on his face.

"Okay, sure! Gosh, I can't wait until I'm older." I laughed, blowing off his concern.

After dinner, Linda and I picked up the plates and cleaned the table. Luckily for me, there was a moment when everyone left the room, and I was alone with the remnants. My mom's and Linda's dad's wineglasses were still half full. I quickly picked each up and drank what was left. *Oh, wow,* I thought. *Red wine is delicious.* It was so different from the tequila we'd had, and I understood why adults had wine each night with dinner.

After my parents said goodnight to Linda's family a few hours later, I lay in bed and realized I hadn't thought about the men in the woods all day. I wondered if the ones who survived were okay. I wondered if they thought of me. I wondered where they were and if I could write to them. I worried that they suffered and would be punished even longer, that it would take them forever to go north like they wanted. I worried they'd never get out. I worried that it was somehow my fault, that I should have told someone they needed help and a place to sleep that night. I worried that someone else would break into our house, someone who didn't know I lived there. The self-confidence I'd felt earlier waned, and panic slipped back in its place. I bit the dried cuticle from the side of my right index finger and thought about what I should do. I knew I couldn't sleep, and the panic was spreading to the pit in my stomach. It was quiet, late. Everyone had gone to bed.

I slipped out of my room and carefully, silently, stepped with slippered feet down the carpeted stairs to the family room. In it stood an enormous antique secretary desk, complete with a cabinet that my mom had restored. It had multiple uses, but the largest and most important role was as my dad's liquor cabinet. Pressing my fingers against the door joint to muffle any sound, I popped open the cabinet and peered inside. Behind the large bottles were smaller airline bottles of booze. A lot of them. I reached in, pulled one out from the back left corner, twisted open the top, and swallowed the contents. It burned and smelled awful, but that warm feeling immediately radiated from my feet and chased away the panic. *It's like medicine*, I thought. Considering and then deciding against taking a second swig, I closed the top and put the bottle back where I'd found it.

Creeping my way back to bed, I softly closed my eyes, realizing how tired I was. But now I knew I could sleep, all bad thoughts and worries having been shut away for the night. I had found a way to feel like myself. At the end of the day, I had found a way to rest.

"So, you started drinking to handle your feelings about what happened to the men you met in the woods, and you found that it worked. You continued to drink to manage your feelings. That is the age where you stopped learning how to deal with your feelings. But you did that because you didn't have support or tools to learn how to deal with your feelings. So, today, as an adult woman, you can choose to do this work to manage your feelings without having to use drugs and alcohol to shut them down."

"Let's explore your beginnings. What kind of schoolgirl were you?"

I tried to be a nice girl. I tried to be good. But there was something inherently wrong with me. There wasn't a time I could remember feeling pleasure. When I wrapped my legs around the horses I rode as a girl, aware of the wind whipping my long, straight hair like a banner as I rode through the fields, I felt numb inside. The feel of my father's chest as I laid my head against it, the pressure of his arms wrapped tight around me in a hug—I knew it was happening. I could feel the sensation of pressure, but the warmth didn't penetrate my heart. Everything inside me felt numb, although I moved through daily life and witnessed my life happening as an outsider.

Nothing felt real to me. I lived as though behind a continual pane of glass. No matter what I tried, I couldn't break through. By all outward appearances, my family looked stable. Economically successful. Homeowners. Living the American suburban dream. But hidden behind the red front door of our lovely home was an unpredictable onslaught of fear and abandonment. My mother's anger grew as my father built his businesses. The rigid control and simmering rage my mother relied on to parent me intensified as the years went on. (I came to understand as I recovered from alcoholism and addiction that the circumstances of my family and my home most likely would not have changed much about my experience. My parents, while struggling with their own issues, tried their best to provide the home, financial support, and opportunities they were denied in their childhoods.)

No matter who I was around or what my circumstances were, I felt different inside. I lacked a sense of myself and tried desperately to fit whatever mold I thought anyone else wanted to see in me. Carly Simon's 1971 song "The Girl You Think You See" spoke to me at a soul level. In it, she describes a girl who longed to know who someone wished her to be, and she would gladly transform into that vision to match that desire. The longing I felt, the pain, and the desire to please whoever stood in front of me was matched perfectly in those desperate lyrics.

I'm eight years old—shy, with straight dark brown, nearly black hair running down my back. I woke each summer day excited to return to the worlds of Tolkien, Lewis, Hans Christian Anderson, Wilder, Christie, and Poe. After breakfast, I'd walk to our screened-in deck off the dining room on the second floor of our house. It was a large addition, lovingly shaded under the branches of tall oak, red maple, and tulip trees. My mother had slowly furnished the deck with wicker treasures brought home each year from their annual trips to Jamaica: a glass-topped coffee table, a sweet sofa, end tables, and a side chair. But the most magnificent piece was the one I claimed: an oversized white wicker rocking chair. Positioned in the near left corner of the deck, I had a grand view of the tree canopy and a full view of the backyard that sloped into the woods. A magical spot where I read four or five books at once, rotating through chapters, easily navigating the storylines as I whiled away the summer days. Getting up only to refill a glass of iced tea, walk the dog, or eat a meal, reading for eight or ten hours a day felt like moments. Disappearing into each world, my heart raced along Frodo's journey, pounded in unison with *The Tell-Tale Heart*, and thrilled with Almanzo as he sledded down the steep snowbanks of upstate New York. With each adventure, I moved further away from my home and only there found relief, joy, and a kind respite from the reality of my daily life.

A sudden, abrupt, sharp command jarringly pulled me back.

"Set the table," my mother ordered from the kitchen.

"One minute, I'm just finishing this chapter," I replied.

Her face hardened as she strode into the deck where I sat reading under the trees. Her dark eyes, just like mine, narrowed. Towering over me, she said, "Give me your book."

I quickly handed it to her, and she confiscated it. "Now, set the table," she growled.

"But it's a library book, and it's due tomorrow! I just want to finish it," I cried, stunned.

"Then you can pay for any late fees out of your allowance," she said, turning back toward the kitchen.

Without thinking, I bit my right index fingernail near the cuticle. Tearing the flesh back a bit, a tiny paper cut-sized red streak widened with blood. Tears sprang up, filling my sockets and threatening to pour forth. But I fought them back. Swallowing, hard, I steadily controlled the upset I felt. Picking the book up from the floor where my mother dropped it, I brushed off the cover and placed it back on the end table with its companions. Waves of sadness, anger, and shame rose and fell like endless tides. I swallowed again, hard, and found that place of numbness. Only then was I ready to cross the threshold back into the house, which was not a home, and do the things I was told to do.

I'm eleven years old. In my room in my second favorite place, at a long white table with a wood top and shelved wicker bottom that served as both a dressing table and desk, I worked on my math homework.

My parents are screaming at each other on the phone. "You better come home tonight, Chuck," my mom yells into the phone. "Don't leave me alone with these girls again," she screams.

Dad's not coming home, Dad's not coming home. In a quiet panic, I moved to the bathroom, the only room with a lock. Carefully pushing the lock button in and muffling the sound, the lock clicked. Sliding down the wall to my left, furthest away from the kitchen, I started rocking, banging my head against the wall. "Nooooo noooo noooo," I moaned, my head picking up speed. I saw a shaving razor on the right corner of the sink and grabbed it, testing its edge against my leg, my arm.

The doorknob jiggled.

"Unlock this door right now, Karen," my mom commanded.

I froze, put the razor back on the counter, stood up, dizzy, and unlocked the door.

My mother leaned over me, her annoyance clearly teetering on anger. "What's the matter with you? Stop making all that racket. You're going to wake your sister. You're just trying to get attention. Now go unload the dishwasher. Then fill a bucket and get a rag. Wash the baseboards in the dining room. You better change your attitude around here, or you'll never see the light of day again."

I'm thirteen years old and busted for smoking in the girls' room at school. Driving me home from the principal's office, my mom yelled, "Your behavior caused me to leave work today. Do you realize that? And smoking? Where did you get those cigarettes? Who gave them to you? If you continue down this path, you're going to end up just like Eric, and he comes from a broken home."

"You know, I'd be fine if I ended up just like Eric. He's my best friend and a better person than you," I defiantly yelled back.

Slamming on the brakes, my mom stopped in the middle of the street and jumped out of the car, pulled open my door, grabbed my arm, yanked me out of the car, and hit me hard across the face. I smirked, wound my arm back as far as I could, and hit her back, hard, across her face. Stunned, mouth agape, my mother gasped, ran back to the car, and left me, victorious, alone in the street.

I was shy. I was bullied in elementary school. When my parents took me out of that Catholic school and put me in public school in the sixth grade, I was hell-bent on not being bullied again.

At St. Bernadette's, ages six and eight

I watched and listened and learned who had the power in the class and was determined to get into that group. And that's how I met Maria and Angie. They were the beautiful girls in school. Maria was a first-generation Italian, sweet, dark, always laughing, gentle, sensual person. Angie, with a wicked sharp tongue and a blond California surfer girl look, was powerful. Both held court in school. Determined not to be bullied again at any cost, I joined in their outer orbit.

It was the seventies. Once, Angie and Maria skipped school and hung out at Angie's condo, drinking all the liquor in the cabinet. While she was waiting outside for Maria's mom to pick her up, Angie suddenly leaned over the front porch railing and vomited all over the concrete steps and shrubbery just below. Despite that gross scene, I was jealous that I wasn't invited. Angie was the epitome of cool and thought I was too straight.

"Do you even smoke weed?" she'd ask, judgment tossed as an afterthought as she turned away.

Maria always defended me; she'd defend anyone. "She can't help it if she's secure in herself! It's not the worst thing, you know, Angie, to have healthy self-esteem and to be a good student."

"I just don't want her to narc us out." Angie's cool gave way to an icy irritation.

"Out of all of us, Karen's probably going on to college to become an attorney. She'll get us all out of everything!" Maria laughed, deep and throaty, a smoker's laugh.

Maria was the perfect blend of style and sweet. I couldn't believe she thought I had self-esteem, thought I was a good student. Grateful for her support, I did anything to remain protected and accepted, or at least ignored. And anytime someone said there was a party or whenever people started hanging out, I'd tag along just to be part of the coolest kids.

There was also my longest friend, June. She was the opposite of those girls: sunny, fun, light, shining, and naturally positive. I had no idea why she liked me, but I was drawn to her. She was everything the other crowd wasn't. She was sure of herself, like she knew herself, but not overconfident or arrogant. She seemed okay with just being who she was: unpretentious, kind, funny, smart, and always helpful, be it a math problem, an argument for an English paper, or just a kind friend who listened. She had a sense of service about her. She was like Anne of Green Gables or Nancy Drew: kind, helpful, light-spirited, eager, and resourceful.

Each weekday morning throughout the school year, I'd walk with June to the entrance gates of school and wait. I'd tell her to go on inside and that I would meet up with her before the bell rang. Maria, Angie, and the rest of the neighborhood girls would all come a few minutes later, close to class start time, and I'd pretend I was tying my shoe or something so it wouldn't be too obvious that I was waiting for them. They'd stop there, form a casual circle, and fire up cigarettes, occasionally passing around a bowl of pot. I remember the first time I saw them do that.

Angie said, "She doesn't smoke," pointing to me.

I said, "Oh yeah, I do," as casually as I could. I continued to wait for them each morning so I could smoke with them. I'd started stealing my mom's cigarettes so I'd have one lit by the time they arrived and then walked into the building as if I belonged to the group.

I guess I did belong, in a way, but I was more on the group's fringes. Angie didn't talk to me much, and I think the others just plain disliked me, but I was friends with Maria. We'd often hang out after school. Her dad was a real hard-ass like my mom, and we had a lot to talk about. We'd sit in her basement, drink a couple of beers, smoke pot, and talk about everything.

Rumors were my specialty.

As the year continued, I drifted away from June and gravitated toward a friendship with Mary, a perennial homecoming court member and cheerleader. Her path to popularity was paved by her three older brothers, successful athletes in baseball and football. Their family was a high school dynasty. Mary was beautiful, kind, humble, and giving. Like June, her spirit was grounded in religion. I learned many years later that she had a strong, active relationship with Jesus, also cultivated by her mother. There was something so open about her spirit; she was always laughing, light, happy, and easily saw the good in others. We spent the summer between our freshman and sophomore year hanging out in her backyard pool, talking and laughing through multiple slumber parties and movies in the theaters. Also, like June, Mary didn't drink, so I hid my drinking from her, sneaking in a few drinks from my parent's liquor cabinet before I met up with her. Only that way could I temporarily ignore the growing pain in my heart and match her carefree demeanor.

As September loomed, Mary's cheerleading practice drew her closer to her squad mates, and she spent less time with me. A slow, dark despair grew in my chest. *She probably figured out that I'm never going to be popular*, I thought. I imagined her suddenly seeing me in a new light, seeing me for who I actually was—selfish, uncoordinated, awkward, homely—and a new villain sprang to life. Jealousy silently slithered in, green tendrils rising from my gut, gently but determinedly twisting a long reach into my heart. *She doesn't appreciate me*, jealousy whispered in my ear. *She's laughing at me, telling her cheerleading squad all the private things I told her.* Insecurity took hold like a misguided life vest, and jealousy, having planted enough seeds in my mind, gave way to anger, masking the gutting abandonment I felt.

More rumors circulated, this time targeting Mary and Stephanie, new best friends on the cheerleading squad.

"Stephanie told the homecoming committee that Mary shouldn't be on the homecoming court because she's butt-ugly and is really a cunt," boys whispered in the hall.

"Mary tried to get Stephanie kicked off cheerleading for drinking," the girls repeated, smirking.

Within a week, people started looking at me differently. The whispers continued now with sideways glances at me when I approached small groups in the school halls. I found myself without a place to sit at lunch; all tables were full, seats saved for kids who never arrived. It slowly dawned on me that I was ostracized, outcast, and rejected. The rumors had been traced back to me, and I had lost all credibility and trust.

By the end of the week, I couldn't take the public isolation and humiliation anymore. I knew people were talking about me, but I didn't know what was being said. Outside the biology lab, I saw Mary approaching for her next class, Stephanie and a few other cheerleaders in tow. I stepped in front of the group.

"Mary. I really want to talk to you," I pleaded.

Stephanie stepped between us.

"Her mother told her she can't talk to you anymore. You're not her friend. Like her mother said, you're a very sick girl. Leave us alone."

And with that, my future in that school was over.

The girls and any hope I had for redemption moved past me in one cohesive movement. Left standing alone in the hall, an icy dread running through my veins, I realized the bell was ringing for the start of class. I entered the classroom alone, in front of everyone, head down, late, a sick loser.

In the spring of my tenth-grade year, we moved fifteen miles and a world away to Vienna, Virginia. What had been my familiar small set of classmates was replaced by an enormous school of mostly wealthy offspring of CEOs, physicians, surgeons, and other white-collar overachievers. BMWs, Oldsmobile Cutlass, Lincolns, and Cadillacs casually spread their cool through the parking lot. Everyone's hair was long, fluffy, and feathered.

My parents approached me about college. My only requirements for college were that it had to have a strong journalism or English program and that it be as far away from home as I could manage to get.

Sitting down with Mrs. Jones, a high school counselor

who had taken an interest in me, my mother began, "Well, you know, we don't have an enormous amount of money. And Karen is certainly not a student. But we do feel we should give her the opportunity to go to college. What she does with that opportunity is up to her. I don't have high hopes," she scoffed. "But she is certainly capable. We did not raise a dummy. I would not tolerate that!"

My father moved his hand on top of hers. "Joanne," he softly chided. "I think what my wife, Karen's mother, means is that we have hopes for her. She has indicated that she's, what, she's interested in English, in journalism. With her grades, which haven't been the best, maybe, but she does have reasonable test scores, where do you think she should apply?"

Mrs. Jones listened intently, taking everything in. "High Point College in North Carolina may be a good option for her. It does have a strong English department and an emerging journalism track, and it is a smaller school. They draw from many students from the Washington, DC, area, so she would have a chance to meet others from similar backgrounds. While it is out of state, her background would make her a good fit for this college. It's one I would recommend."

I had wanted to go to Northwestern for journalism (too far) or the University of Richmond (too expensive), but High Point, North Carolina, seemed far enough that my parents couldn't just drive over on a whim. It was a different world. Plus, it had a strong English department, which was good enough for me. So, in August 1980, we packed all the things I felt were too important to leave behind: blue jeans, an assortment of T-shirts, my favorite sweatshirt, hiking shoes, all my books and vinyl records, and my prized silver Technics record player carefully wrapped in brown packing paper and burlap. Everything fit into the brass-handled footlocker trunk my mother insisted on purchasing. All I cared about fit into

4.13 cubic feet, with room to spare. We piled into my dad's black Chevy Cavalier and drove down the interstate, past Kings Dominion theme park, through notable Civil War and Revolutionary War towns: Petersburg, Warfield, and South Hill, crossing over the North Carolina border past Henderson and into college basketball territory, finally entering High Point, proudly designated as the Furniture Capital of the World on the welcome sign at the town border.

Months passed. I settled into a routine with my roommate, Liz, whose New Jersey Italian accent got butchered by the North Carolina drawl she couldn't help but pick up. I found my way into a staff reporter spot covering sports for the Hi-Po, the school newspaper. I also secured the midnight to 4 a.m. slot spinning records on 90.5 WWIH, the local radio station, bringing New York and British punk to the rednecks of North Carolina.

I'd get off around predawn, around 4:15 every morning, and head over to the music director Rick's house a block off campus. Perpetually hopped up on speed, Rick would cook me breakfast, and we'd play backgammon until our 8 a.m. classes.

Indian summer painted an easy autumn. Days were spent outdoors, sunbathing well into October, watching the frat boys toss frisbees in the Quad. Years later, my mother gave me a box of remembrances, and in it, I found my first letter home from college, full of optimism and hope.

"Why did you get so angry when Kathy said she was from High Point?" Charles probed.

"I went to college for a year at High Point College. It was a terrible, bad place. Full of townies, rednecks, and hicks, even in the college itself. There weren't a lot of people who understood me or my roommate because we were 'Northerners,' or worse, 'Yankees.' The classes were okay, but the people were awful. I didn't fit in. I spent most of the time drinking and drugging my way through that year. But I can't tell you what happened. I can't talk about it."

"There's a saying in the Program," Charles gently offered. "You're only as sick as your secrets. Keeping secrets about who you are, what you've done, and what's happened to you keeps you trapped in shame and fear. What you have here is a way out of that. Do you want a way out?" He held out his hand.

Something about the gentleness he offered and the depth of his understanding made me hesitate. I'd never told anyone about that year in college. But Charles was making space for me to talk about it. And even though I didn't know him, I felt an unexplainable trust in him. It's like he knew what I would say, but he couldn't say it for me. Shame had always held me back; it infused the air I breathed every day for as long as I could remember. For the first time, I considered what he offered: *What would I be like if I wasn't filled with shame and fear?*

I saw his hand still outstretched. I realized I'd been looking down for a long time. Looking up, I met his eyes, steady and ready.

"Okay," I said. "But I don't want to talk here. I don't want to look at you. Can we go outside? Can I talk to you while we go on a walk?"

"Yes," he said as he gently motioned toward the door.

It's still sunny, I thought, breathing in the warm October breeze filled with the scent of camellia, cosmos, lilies, and asters. Turning toward the lake, Charles at my side, I took a deeper breath and began.

I wanted to study English when I went to college. In my favorite English class sat a boy who caught my eye. He was tall, blond, tortured, and sensitive. He was beautiful, with long, straight hair and the greenest eyes I've ever seen. Serious-faced, he stood weekly and read poems straight from his pierced heart. My breath stopped when he read; I felt he turned a key in my heart. I couldn't speak, and I would never speak of the stir he caused my spirit from his words. No matter the assignment, he stood at some point during class to read a poem. Each week, a different poem. He was prolific, sensitive, and intense. I'd never seen anyone so brave. I had been writing things down for years that I fiercely kept private, yet here he was, standing up in class without embarrassment or hesitation, reading his most personal writings. It blew me away, and I fell wildly in love with him from the distance of twenty chairs.

He didn't know me, didn't see me. We never spoke. But as each weekend ended, bringing Monday's class so close, I felt a quiet excitement that was new to me. *What would he read this week?* I wondered. So focused on the thrill of his new words, I barely remembered my assignment, finishing it as an afterthought, as my ticket into his event that I craved.

Besides having a love of English, I was passionate about music and found an opportunity to join the college radio station as a graveyard shift DJ. I made it my quiet mission to bring this small town of hicks into the twenty-first century and enlighten them with East Coast and British New Wave and punk music. It was my favorite job, spinning records.

The station itself was in the tower of Roberts Hall. Around 8 p.m. on Tuesdays and Thursdays, I'd pack up two lugging duffel bags full of LPs, sling each over a shoulder, and carry them from my room in Millis, down Extraordinary Way, and cut across the grass to Roberts. Entering the stately building, I'd schlep myself and my vinyl treasure up two massive stairways, open the door to the Tower, and, grasping the iron railing, climb another flight up the spiral staircase. Out of breath, I'd take a moment and then enter WWIH, 90.5. I'd get a Coke from the dorm-style refrigerator near the reception desk, make myself comfortable on the musty, overstuffed, broken-springed couch, open the duffels, and order the records according to that evening's playlist I had in my mind: Duran Duran, Spandau Ballet, the Human League, ABC, Depeche Mode. It was satisfying, solitary, and creative, just how I most liked spending my time.

One night when I was on the radio, I took a call. It was that poet boy-man.

He liked my music. He said he noticed my smile in class. He said he was having a party and that I should stop by when I got off my shift.

"It'll be too late," I said. "I don't get off until two a.m. tonight."

"You'll be right on time," he said, sending goosebumps down my neck with the warmth in his voice.

I was stunned. I didn't know he noticed me or knew who I was. Giddy like a Disney princess, I finished out the last set and, an hour later, packed my records up. Figuring I could pick them up the next day after class, I left them in a corner with a note on top: "Karen's—picking up tomorrow."

I entered his dorm. *It's so quiet*, I thought, but then again, it was the middle of the night. I knocked softly on his door, and he answered. There was no one else visible in his room.

"Oh!" I exclaimed. "I'm sorry I'm so late. Where is everybody? I missed the party." Embarrassed, I turned to leave.

"Wait a minute," he said, reaching for my arm. "You're fine. Everybody will be back soon. Some people went to get more beer, ice, and drinks. Don't worry, come on in."

Something didn't feel right. I suddenly felt unsure of what was happening. Something felt off, but I couldn't name it; it was just outside my inner knowing.

I turned again to leave, and his grip tightened on my arm.

"You know, I'm kind of tired," I said.

"Come here, girl," he said, pulling me off-center. I stepped to steady myself and realized I had stepped inside the door. He picked up a red plastic cup from the desk beside the door.

"Drink this," he said, smiling, eyes cold.

I felt confused. "Uh, no thanks," I said, feeling wary. "I think I'll just go home."

He stared me down. "You're not going anywhere." His voice was hard and hollow, like a steel pipe.

He stretched out his arms, his wide hands opening like the mouth of a bulldozer, fingers like the forked ends. Staring, not believing what was happening, time moving in slow motion, I was lifted in the air and flew, flew silently across the room, like a cloud, like rain, like fluff from a shredded toy, and landed, *whoosh*, on the mattress of the top bunk. His face over mine, huge, his tongue licking my neck, my cheek over my shut lips. "Kiss me," he ordered, choking out the command in a deep, thick, gravelly voice.

I turned my face, wriggling. I realized I was screaming because my throat hurt. He flipped me over, and then I was on top. *Oh god, he's making me do this from on top.*

Why isn't anyone coming? Why isn't anyone here?

Things I remember: him pressing me down from under my hips, tongue down my throat, making me say I love you, making me do things to him.

I can't get out.

I was screaming, and nobody came.

Things I don't remember: most of what happened, leaving, going back to my dorm.

Waking up, my roommate shook me awake.

"You have to get up," she said. "You have to. You can't just let him win."

Confused, I shook my head, trying to remember. "What are you talking about?"

"You don't remember? Early this morning, it was still dark out. Our dorm room door flew open and banged against the wall, scared the crap out of me. You were just standing there, crying. Standing and crying in a ripped shirt. Your shirt was ripped right in half, straight down the middle, and you were holding it closed with your right hand. You were shaking, and you told me everything that happened."

"I don't remember what happened."

"You did, right when you came in. And I told you we needed to report it, but you said no. You just wanted a shower. All you wanted was a shower, and you started shouting, 'Shower!' So, I helped you get undressed and down the hall to get cleaned up. Your arms are bruised. Do you see that?"

They were. Big, black, and burgundy bruises on my upper arms.

I was so tired. Really, really tired.

"I'm going to sleep for a while," I told her. Really, I wanted to curl up and be left alone.

"Are you sure you're okay?" she asked.

"Yes, I swear. I'm not going anywhere," I tried reassuring her. My voice sounded hollow. I felt hollow.

"Okay, I'm going to class, but I'll come back and check on

you," my roommate said.

It's so hard to remember. It's hard to know what really happened.

I don't know why I was so frozen. It's hard to explain why I didn't just leave. Something was terrifying, and I had this experience of entering a dissociated state. I was feeling myself leaving my body, leaving, leaving, but I couldn't move my body. It was a place where time slowed down, like in a movie, like Alice falling down the rabbit hole, and I was screaming but couldn't hear it. I just knew it from the pain in my throat. And I can't explain the terror, that insidious terror that snuck up like a shadow, a shadow that darkened and enveloped me from the ground up as I realized what was happening, but it couldn't be happening, because this just doesn't happen. So how can I explain it because it doesn't make sense? I don't remember. I just know the feeling, and I said his name every day when I woke up for the next thirty years.

I told people he pulled a knife on me, and that's why I was afraid to turn and run.

But the truth is I don't remember.

So I did what I always do and put that thing in a box, in a locked place inside of me, and tried to go to class. I wrote a few articles in the school newspaper.

But I was scared that he ruined sex for me, that I'd never have a normal experience again, and so at night, I wandered. I wandered the campus and found different guys to go home with. I told myself that I was going to have sex until it felt better, until it felt okay, until it felt good. One third-year student on the football team played center and was huge, had huge arms, a huge chest, and thick, curly hair. He was kind. I don't know why I chose him, but I did. I'd knock softly at the back door of his off-campus apartment. He'd let me in. Wordlessly, I'd walk quietly to his bed and lay down, moving to lay my head on his chest. We never spoke, and he always let me stay. I don't know that I knew his name; I just knew I needed to feel safe, and he let me. He gave me that kindness and asked for nothing in return.

I stopped going to the radio station, and I stopped going to classes. Most nights, I drank at parties, townie bars, or in my room. My roommate and I made furniture out of beer cans. By April, I had stopped talking altogether and went home to my parents' house back in Vienna, defeated and ashamed. But I couldn't tell them what happened because I didn't understand what had happened. I couldn't remember, even though I knew. Deep down, I knew. I decided I needed a plan B for my life—and a good one at that.

Trauma work is so important. Years and years later, I learned that this event in college was rape. I had just thought I was stupid and had put myself in that position, going to a guy's room by myself late at night. I thought I deserved it. I thought it was too far in the past to do any sort of therapy on it, so I just stuck it in the back of my mind (even though I never forgot about it). About a decade and a half passed, and I was in counseling for something else and mentioned it, sort of as a throwaway comment, stopping my therapist cold. She immediately pivoted and asked me if I would be willing to try eye movement desensitization and reprocessing (EMDR), an incredible technique for healing trauma going back to childhood. Highly recommend. Another level of healing, all from telling someone the truth.

Compassion

One of the key skills I developed during my treatment was an ability to listen. There was so much in me that raged just below my smiling surface, but in joining the treatment groups and going to the mandatory meetings, I learned that I simply couldn't dominate the floor. People took turns talking, giving me ample time to practice listening.

At first, it all sounded like whining to me. I entered this "practice" perpetually annoyed and impatient for my turn to talk. My abdomen became a boiling cauldron of the worst witch's brew: anger, jealousy, rage, and blame mixed with a strong base of fear. Unable to name what I was feeling, I only felt panicky at this mess inside me, threatening to boil over in some uncontrollable way. I was unaware that the time I spent waiting for my turn to talk was a gentle introduction to sitting with myself, sitting with my feelings, and listening to the whiners. I slowly learned how to turn my attention from that boiling mess inside me to what someone else was saying. I learned how to endure their sharing without rolling my eyes.

The bulk of the treatment center patients were what I would consider rednecks: White, uneducated, at least in terms of their exposure to anything outside of their immediate world and generation. Rough. Blue-collar working stock, which I equated with low intelligence, nonthinking types. Stubborn, set in their ways, bigoted, racist. Limited people, the type of people who, later in life, I would secretly, shamefully, categorize as "the reality TV crowd." People who made me cringe at the thought of being part of their same species. I didn't want to know them, understand them, relate to them, or feel any kinship or compassion for them. What was their point other than mindlessly reproducing, filling caretaking roles, or fixing things? I looked down at any profession that seemed mindless—in other words, anything using your hands. I figured people ended up in those professions because they weren't smart enough to do anything else. In sharing space with them, I felt shame for us both. My fortressed brain, with limited knowledge and a black-and-white binary perspective, judged harshly.

 I had a picture in my mind of who I thought I was and who I was supposed to be. As far back as I could remember, I held this image in my mind, and I always fell short. As a young girl with what I laughingly brushed off as "a custom set of legs God created just for me," I was physically awkward. My left hip had undergone several surgeries, leaving me with a wide, Frankenstein-like scar that sprung several inches above my bikini line. My knees betrayed me, dislocating at the slightest provocation. And my right leg was a half inch longer than my left, which I compensated for by walking on the ball of my left foot. My gait was noticeably different. Because I had missed so many physical development milestones, many of which I wasn't aware of until I had children of my own and watched their development, I was not socialized well. People my age terrified me. I became comfortable and confident performing amazing feats of memorization for my parents' friends—attorneys, budding CEOs, real estate developers—during the many happy hours held at our home. I learned executive speak and how to overcome performance anxiety long before I knew how to make a friend my own age.

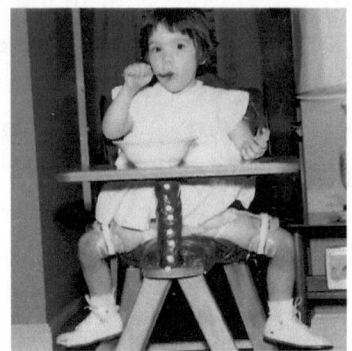 

In leg braces (left) and body cast (right)

Even before we knew about my legs, I suffered from a steady stream of ear infections as a baby. The most popular treatment at that time was repeated rounds of Tetracycline. No one knew the permanent damage it caused to my adult teeth, which were years from emerging. The dark stains at the gum line, extending to about half of each tooth, delighted the popular Catholic schoolgirls who had a wickedly creative selection of cruel nicknames for me.

I felt different, and I was different. I thought I was alone with my defects, my obviously weird body. And then puberty hit, and my face and back erupted with acne—terrible, pizza face acne.

Who would ever love me? I thought, crying in my pillow night after night. I was filled with self-loathing, loathing for anyone who didn't fit this ambiguous picture I held onto of middle- and upper-class success, loathing for my family, so cold and empty. Those airline mini bottles of booze I returned to night after night offered the only solution to silence the constant stream of self-loathing running through my head. By sixteen, I couldn't sleep without sneaking a few mixed drinks. At first, I was terrified of getting caught by my parents, but over time, I realized they weren't paying enough attention to notice.

I settled into a nightly routine: clean the dinner table (walk through the formal living room to the bar and take a drink), do the dishes (take another drink), finish my homework (slipping a mini in my pocket so I could get through that task), wash my face and brush my teeth, and say good nights to my parents (and walk through the formal living room to the bar and take another drink). Outside my teenage awareness, alcohol had found ripe ingredients in my angst, and the kicker was our far-reaching family genetics, going back, way back before Virginia, before Maryland, before my great-grandfather arrived in Boston, back generations to our origins in Ireland. I carried it all within me, and by the time I reached seventeen, I had honed a daily maintenance dependence on alcohol that would rival any stressed-out middle-aged executive.

In treatment, I listened and found pockets of truths coming from the lips of those older redneck men and women I wanted to loathe so much. Slowly, haltingly, painful histories slipped out during our group meetings, in line as we waited for the transport van to take us to outside meetings, in casual one-line jokes that revealed a darker truth during dinners. Three weeks away from alcohol and cocaine, my brain stayed a little longer in a conversation or two. Fewer jagged random thoughts were darting in and out like manic squirrels. As I started hearing and listening more clearly, I heard myself in more of their snippets and stories.

Before she graduated from treatment, I sat in the main hall one night with one of my suitemates. We rocked in the old rockers on the front porch and watched a crescent moon rise over the trees.

"You know I was married before this one," she started.

"No, I didn't know that," I replied.

"My daddy used to tell me I wouldn't be good for anything 'cept for popping out kids, and I'd better get at it right after high school before my face wrinkled."

"That's awful." It sounded a little too much like something my mother would say to me.

"Oh yeah, that was nuthin'. He'd have me come down to the shop on the weekends, and he'd sit back behind that big dirty counter and stare out at the workshop. He'd point at one or two of the guys and tell me to take something over to them just to see if anyone took another look at me. He was so busy trying to get me off his hands before I got too old. It was like a window closing on my life. And I knew I'd never go to college. I'd just end up married to the first one who would have me, like my mom. And look at how he whittled her down to nuthin', you know? She's just broken, her heart's just broken, and it's all she could do to just keep us alive. So, I married the first one who took me, but you know, it didn't last. It didn't last at all."

That feeling. Oh, my gosh, that feeling of being so worthless that your family couldn't wait to get rid of you, make you somebody else's problem. Her beauty didn't save her, didn't give her the things she wanted. It didn't matter. She was shattered from the inside out, just like me.

I looked at her again, wide-eyed. Here she was, about to graduate. Older, with a better marriage, two kids, and starting from the same place I was at. I felt a sameness between us, and neither one of us had to say anything else. I knew she felt it too, in how she looked at me. She looked away and then squeezed my hand.

"You're gonna be all right, baby girl," she said and left me rocking in the night with that shining crescent moon.

I slowed down. I took more walks outside with that bluegrass-picking yodeler from deep in South Carolina. We'd sit by the pond, and he'd listen to me talk, peeling back the crusty bandages I'd placed over all my inner wounds, one by one. He listened, and he'd pick his guitar, and when I said something particularly revealing or real, he'd let out a loud yodel like I'd never heard before. It was the most beautiful reward. He gave me safety and space, and as I settled in the grass next to him and his music, I looked more closely at his face and his hands. Rough, tanned, lined from years of hard work in a factory. He drank out of habit and mostly boredom, with a bit of heartbreak thrown in. He was so handsome, patient, and kind, and I loved him with everything in me, all at once. Then he told me about the night his father hanged himself out in the garage after his business closed, the accidents he saw in the factory, the terrible mistakes that cost men their fingers or worse, and the day his wife and daughter died in a flood. He held so much and had held so much in. Those lines—not as dirty anymore, but the pain he held—marked the strength and the dignity that held him up as long as they could until he was full, and it all just let go. I saw in that man, that deep Southern man, who didn't judge anyone but just quietly picked his guitar and saw everything, the wisdom and knowledge and pain and beauty of humanity. Shame washed over me from all the judgment I had held, and I knew it was nothing but fear. And we all had that fear in different ways. We were all there because the only way we'd found to keep that fear, shame, and loathing at bay was to ingest large quantities of chemicals, and they'd just stopped working for all of us. Just as I'd seen with my suitemate, he and I were the same too. He gave out a long yodel and stroked my hair. He saw me, and I let him. For a moment, my heart blew open, and I felt alive in a way I'd never felt.

"You're going to have to look for ways of relating in," Charles advised me. "You're young, but you've already been through a lot of things that people you'll meet will be talking about. Listen for the feelings," he encouraged me. "You have a really big heart, and you'll have no problems finding people who understand what you've gone through, if you tell the truth about who you are."

Oh. *That's all I have to do?* I thought. I'd never really told anyone who I was. I'd been lying so long, I wasn't sure I knew the truth anymore. I mean, it was all about figuring out who people wanted me to be and giving them that version as best I could. That's how our family worked. But somehow, his words got into the back of my mind, and I started opening up more in meetings, inside the treatment center, and in outside meetings. I started letting the anger out, cussing people out when they said things I thought were dishonest or, worse, stupid. I cried in frustration at not being able to express myself. Here's the weird part, though: no one reprimanded me. No one even responded in any way other than to come to me after the meeting to hug me. My pain opened avenues for other people to start talking about their pain, and their pain did the same for me. Rivers of emotion flowed each night. I saw myself in everyone, and their lives had worth, so much worth, so much purpose. The care they gave to others, to me, blew my mind.

Decades later, as my marriage failed, my finances failed,

and my plans failed, I turned to a profession I never thought I'd engage in. To make money to feed my kids, within a month of my marriage ending, I opened a home day-care business and took on the care of six kids under the age of three. Grueling, hard, physically and emotionally demanding work for very little money, but it was enough to get us on our feet that first year. And I received patronizing contempt from the parents of the children I cared for. It was mostly hidden but always floating in the air. They pitied me, the same way I'd pitied and loathed people who struggled in service or blue-collar work years before. I knew then that the people I'd once judged so harshly as not being "smart enough" to cut it in higher-paying professions were brilliantly creative, savvy in ways of survival and societal navigation I'd only just started learning about, some of the most critical people in our society. They were deemed the "essential workers" during the COVID-19 pandemic, which included not only medical staff but the supporting service workers who kept the economy moving and took care of the children of the medical teams so they could, in turn, care for the sickest COVID patients. Those humans kept things moving when no one else could. They deserve our greatest respect, compensation, gratitude, and care. And it was only from learning how to listen and relate to feelings and to walk the daily grind of setting up six playpens, changing dozens of diapers daily, and feeding six wildly entitled toddlers that the truth landed in my bones. I learned how to forgive myself for my unfair bias and judgment of others, forged from years of fear. Freedom from fear and the long, slow relinquishment of self-judgment led to freedom from the compulsion to judge others. I no longer needed to protect myself by "othering" people. When I open myself to the humanity clearly before me, I can clearly see the grace that surrounds us all.

In treatment, I learned about a new framework for living. You can have goals, sure, but the trick is to live each day fully and not worry about the future. Or the past, for that matter. It's the whole Ram Dass *Be Here Now* thing, Thich Nhat Hanh's mindfulness orientation, or the multiple ways to discipline my mind using a one-day-at-a-time approach. It made no sense to me. Everything in my life was either on fire or charred beyond recognition. Family? Hated me. Friends? What friends? Job and income? On life support. Credit? Destroyed for at least another seven to ten years, based on all the collections and overwhelming debt I'd racked up. Health? Uh, I was in treatment with an angry liver and a mind compulsively mainlining anxiety. Housing? Nonexistent. I was so overwhelmed that I couldn't figure out where to start. Every second, I heard an emergency alarm system going off in my head. Like an air raid siren from World War II, a siren slowly wound up, *Wwrrrrrrraaaeeeiiii*, gradually increasing volume, sound speeding up and ending with people screaming. My everyday personal playlist.

Along with taking each day as it comes, I learned about paying attention to my body, which, up until then, I'd only looked at, in passing, with deep loathing. My body had never been a comfortable, happy place to be. When I looked at it, I saw big thighs, a much too large rear, and all the places that had been broken. I'd never considered how I physically felt, though. Was I hungry? I don't know. Was I feeling angry? Yes, all the time. How about lonely? Of course. I'd been lonely my entire life, and I walled up in an ice-rimmed cylinder that ran through my inside core. Finally, was I tired? Oh my gosh, yes. Trying to look like you know what you're doing when you're falling apart from the inside out is exhausting.

"That HALT acronym means don't get too hungry, angry, lonely, or tired," Charles explained. Well, I was all those things—all the time. However, if I combined framework part one (take this day as it comes) with part two (HALT), it might be possible to figure out how to navigate all this.

I realized I was hungry, so I drummed up a small snack. Angry? Write about it, which honestly felt like the worst thing to do. I could also scream, hit something (preferred), or talk it out with someone, which could, in theory, start addressing the lonely part. And tired? I was always tired. My body wasn't adjusting well to staying awake without cocaine. I was prescribed naps, which I'd never allowed myself to enjoy. Naps were for infants and the elderly—again, nonproductive (or unimportant) people. But while I was in treatment, I conceded to the wisdom of Charles the Counselor and took at least one nap each day.

It made sense that because I didn't know I was an alcoholic and an addict, I didn't consider how physical the impacts of alcoholism and addiction were, as well as the traumas I had experienced. *The Body Keeps the Score* talks about the traumas that stay in your body throughout your life. Considering everything my body had been through, it was no surprise that I concluded that life on the physical plane was not comfortable, pleasurable, or safe. It was no wonder I'd wanted to spend as much time not here as possible.

"Write down your history," Charles instructed. "Make it easy on yourself. Start from your first memories. What do you remember? What happened? Who was there? What did you feel like? What happened next?"

Again, not what I had in mind or wanted to do. But I didn't have anything else to do, so I began to write it all down. Two themes appeared. One, I had a crappy life so far in my physical body and felt betrayed by it. Two, the pattern of seeking my mother's love and approval, getting rejected, and then avoiding her altogether or doubling down on my efforts permeated all of my relationships. By honestly putting these memories and thoughts down on paper in a sort of timeline format, I revealed how much had happened to me that wasn't my fault. Somewhere along the line of my earliest years, I'd started expecting myself to know everything, know how to act and respond like an adult. I'd not permitted myself to be a child, and seeing everything written, I saw how much had happened to me in childhood. I'd expected to be a fully formed adult in a smaller body.

"Write down the times you had fun too," Charles added.

That was harder—much harder. Was it because I held a negative bias? Was I simply choosing not to remember the positives? Trying to figure this out on my own proved infuriatingly impossible. I had to talk it through to find my way back into memories.

"I know I had a friend in kindergarten, but she moved away after that school year ended. I think we had fun together. And then Linda and I were friends for several years and would get into these outrageous giggling fits, so we must have been having a good time. But I didn't have close friends in early elementary school; I was bullied by the popular girls—one girl named April, who sat in front of me, and her friend Nancy. There was another really tall redheaded girl whose name escapes me. I felt lonely and scared and kind of sick to my stomach about spending day after day, year after year, with those girls.

"One of the most humiliating memories of those early

years was when my mom wanted to throw a birthday party for me, so she invited all of those girls over to the house. I begged her not to, but she wanted me to try to make friends with them and thought that would help. I remember them laughing at my home and making snobby remarks about it. There was some talk afterward about how desperate I was to have friends that I made my mom invite over everybody, which, of course, wasn't true. That may have been when I learned how powerful rumors can be. I started studying them.

"By the time we were all in the fifth grade, I couldn't take it anymore. April was sitting in front of me in class, and it was very quiet, as Catholic school classrooms tend to be. She wasn't particularly pretty; I wasn't sure what the draw was about her or how she could hang around the popular girls so easily. Her freckled, round, moon-shaped face held big, round, brown eyes and thin lips. Her tight brown braids fell on either side of her head, just behind her ears.

"She was whispering something about me to another girl sitting to her right. I heard her say my name and laugh lightly. I couldn't take it another moment. Five straight years of being mocked, and I was done. It no longer mattered what would happen, how I would be punished or forever doomed. Taking her braids in each of my hands, I grasped tight and slowly pulled her head backward until her ear was next to my lips.

"'If you don't like me, why don't you just ignore me?' I growled. Giving her braids a quick tug for emphasis, I let her go.

"It all happened in the briefest moment. She looked down and back at me over her left shoulder, wide-eyed and hesitant, for once unsure of herself. The nun hadn't even seen what happened, and I knew I was in the clear. Power surged through my middle, down my arms, and out my hands. I thought lightning bolts would burst out from my palms. I felt powerful, invincible, and quietly exhilarated. From that moment on, they no longer bothered me, and I finished the school year with an unfamiliar, quiet state of being unbothered."

Why do some people stay in your mind? It's been decades since that time of my life, and I still remember April, although her sting is gone. At that moment, when I reached the "I can't take it anymore" place, an inner badass rose in me. April was the girl on my path who summoned my inner badass. Without her, I may not have met my inner warrior. That warrior side believed in me, thought I was worthy of being championed and stood up for. And invoking her to take on the mean girls felt way more possible than taking on my mom.

Thinking about how to apply HALT required me to think about my body, which was a place I never wanted to be and remembered only as an afterthought. Being clean and sober gave me time and space to start thinking about why I felt that way, why I'd never felt at home in my body.

"You know, Charles," I started during another one-on-one therapy session. "I didn't even find out that I'd broken my collarbone until a guy was kissing me one summer night. He ran his finger down my neck, traced my clavicle, and pulled back. 'Why does your left collarbone stick out more than your right?' he asked me.

"'I don't know!' And that's when I realized that something must have happened, but I didn't know what."

"How did you find out that it was actually broken?" Charles asked, his curiosity clearly captured.

"Well, the next time I went to see the orthopedist—you know, I had regular appointments because of my knees—I asked him what he thought. And he said it was probably one of the times I broke my left arm that I also broke my collarbone. Thinking back, it was probably when I fell out of my favorite tree in the backyard. I had just missed falling on the cement patio by inches, and it was a terrible break on my wrist. In fact"—I paused, offering my left hand to Charles—"you can see it never healed right. If I straighten my arm, my left hand dips down to the right, and if I hold my right hand level, you see how my arm twists to the left. See?" I showed him my wrist, and his eyebrows raised a smidge.

"So, between the hip surgeries I had as a kid, all the years my knees dislocated, the eventual knee surgeries, the broken arms, my nasty Tetracycline-stained teeth, and then, as if that wasn't enough, all the bullying, the sexual assaults, and my lack of coordination and inability to walk and run like other kids—well, yeah, being here on Planet Earth, in this body, just wasn't a really fun experience for me."

"Let's go for a walk," Charles said gently but firmly, as was his way, and we left his office and walked around the pond again.

"It's nice out," he pointed out. "It's the perfect temperature out here for me. How does it feel to you?" Charles didn't know that he was giving me a way to access the physical world that would become, years later, crucial to my survival as I faced the most dangerous threat I would ever meet.

I paused, realizing that I wasn't truly aware we were outside. My mind was still drifting through my past, remembering how lonely and weird I had felt in my life. I looked up and saw sunrays sparkling between the tree leaves just overhead, branches softly and slowly waving in the light breeze.

"It's nice," I said, thinking about the sun.

"Stop thinking. Stop walking. Close your eyes. What do you hear?"

I stopped. Closing my eyes, I took a breath and listened.

"The breeze. It's moving the tree branches. A little traffic on the road. It sounds like somebody's radio is on in the distance."

"Good, good. Okay, now try this. What do you feel?"

What do I feel? Hmm. Warm. The sun is warm.

"I feel the sun on my face, my neck, my arms. It's warm, but the air is just slightly cool. It's nice."

"Okay. Open your eyes. What do you see?"

I took a sharp breath in. Charles. He had the warmest gray eyes I had ever seen. Thick, wavy, brown hair curled down his neck a bit. And he really saw me. He was standing in front of me, studying my face. I felt flushed and looked away.

"I see . . . I see . . ." I stammered, eyes darting to land on something that wasn't him. "Okay, well, the pond, of course. And the leaves are starting to show a bit of color, gold, a bit of brown, a few turning orangey. There's a couple of people walking around the far-left side of the pond."

"Great! You're starting to see some details that I bet you missed before you paid attention. Now take a breath. What do you smell?"

I wanted to lean in and smell his scent. Instead, I took a deep breath and tasted what I smelled.

"It's clean, the air here. It's cool and crisp. It smells like fall. It's different from summer. I can't explain it."

"Okay. Now let's sit down. Right on the ground. Okay, turn around and lean against my back. Good. Now what do you feel?"

Are you serious, Charles? I feel horny, like I want to

jump on you right this second. Cut it out, I commanded my needy girl brain. *Okay, pay attention. What do I feel?*

"The ground. My hands are on the ground, and it feels, uh, earthy. And your back. I can feel you breathing against my back. My tush is getting cold. But it feels good, like I could sit here for a while." That was as close as I could get to naming what I really felt.

"I feel you supporting me," Charles said. "We're supporting each other. And that's what recovery is about. You being willing to be supported and to support your new friends in recovery."

I don't want new friends in recovery. I wanted Charles, and if I couldn't have him, then I wanted the guitar-picking yodeler. I wanted to bury my face in a man and soak him all in. But Charles wanted me to pay attention to my own experience, and I wasn't used to that. I was like a girl-toy who sat in a little box somewhere until someone pushed a button that turned me on so I could focus entirely on them. That's when I came alive.

"I want you to practice this every day," Charles said, looking at me. "It's called a Five Senses practice. So, every day, I want you to go outside for a walk and pay attention to what you see, smell, hear, feel, and taste (you can do that part when you're eating a meal or a snack if you'd like). Over time, you'll get used to being in touch with your body, which will help you get in touch with all of you and trust your feelings."

"I don't trust myself, though," I protested. "I mean, I do a lot better when I just do what people like you tell me to do."

"I know. I understand. But this is how you'll discover who you really are and how to get to know the wonderful woman I see right in front of me. You're going to be fine—really! I think you're going to make it because even though this is hard work, what I'm asking you to do, you're willing to do it.

You don't run away."

I wasn't sure I would make it. I didn't want to think about the future. I just wanted to stay right there, with Charles believing in me and me believing in him. I didn't know that what he was teaching me would offer me the greatest healing and become the most challenging pathway for my growth for the remainder of my days.

Forgiveness

"I'm scared to leave," I confessed as my treatment center crush gently plucked the strings of his guitar the Saturday before I was scheduled to return to Washington. We were sitting in our usual spot under a tulip poplar tree in the western corner of the pond behind the cafeteria.

"Oh, you're gonna be okay. I just know it," he murmured, eyes focused on his guitar pick.

"I can't lose this feeling of being such a loser. I just failed in every area of my life, you know? I don't want to face my family; I just can't. I let my sister and my dad down so hard."

He looked up and leaned in close to my face. Putting his guitar down, he brushed a wisp of hair that had fallen over my brow and ran the back of his fingers down the right side of my face. "Girl, listen to me. You've done nothing more than any of us in here have done, and you got out of that life so much faster than most. You gotta let all that go. You know, it's done, and it's over. It's all over. You're going to leave here and live this life full of dreams and goodness and giving. You're going to help so many people. You're a beautiful woman, you've got so much ahead of you that's good, and you just don't see it yet. But I see it. I see it in you."

Turning my head so he wouldn't see the tears filling my eyes, I brushed my lips in the palm of his hand that caressed me. His words washed over me, but I couldn't absorb them, no, not yet. He was too generous, too kind, and I felt I didn't deserve his attention, much less his kindness. But he saw a future in me that I couldn't grasp; it was too much to hope for. I stood up and ran back inside.

Returning to my room, holding back the tears that continued to threaten a state of overflow, I flopped down on my bed. Restlessly, I flipped onto my side and reached for the first book on the pile scattered next to my bed. *Oh, great. Of course*, I thought. *It would have to be the Big Book of Alcoholics Anonymous*. Tears drying rapidly as an irritable mood arose, I did what I always did when I didn't know what to read: fanned the pages until I landed on a random spot to begin. I opened to the chapter on Step Eleven. I read the clear instructions about how each night I was to review my day, noting when I had been selfish, dishonest, fearful, or resentful, which, in my habitual way of looking at the world, showed up as blaming others or feeling jealous. I thought about whether I owed anyone an apology and whether I'd been completely truthful. I looked at the day I'd just spent and tried to name any times when I'd been helpful to someone else. Nope. I'd pretty much been worried about leaving—scared, in fact—and ran away from the one person who offered kindness to me. Clearly, I could own that behavior and circle back with an apology. There was much work I needed to do to feel less afraid.

Reading further, I thought, *Ugh. There's that mention of God again*. I cringed. I just couldn't be part of the whole God thing; it was an immediate turnoff. It tapped a real fear that I wouldn't be able to get clean and sober if it all meant I had to become some God person. Charles had tried to explain to me that the references to God didn't at all mean religion, but it felt like a tricky manipulation to me—and suspiciously cult-like. But there was something there, in that passage, that kept me thinking and invited a hint of curiosity. *I do think of myself most of the time*, I admitted to myself internally, alone, in that room. *I am selfish.* I continued my review without realizing what I was doing. *I am afraid, always.*

Reading on, I saw clear directions for how to begin each day.

Before automatically moving into my day, the book suggested that I should first pray or ask God to remove self-pity, dishonesty, or self-seeking motives (which I interpret as self-obsession) from my thinking. After I simply ask for that, apparently, it's okay to trust my thinking from that moment forward. That mental shift, a gift from God, is supposed to have happened. Just like that. Sounded dubious to me, but I thought, *Well, maybe I should give that a shot.* After all the ways I'd blown up my life and all the bad judgment I'd exercised in the past, I didn't have much trust in my own thinking. But I also didn't have much more to lose.

Here's the clincher. This part of the eleventh step closes with the instruction that we can then simply relax. "Easy does it," or so the slogan advises. I didn't know anything about relaxing. That's what the booze was for, right? As I muddled through this passage, it came to me that trust was what was lacking. I didn't trust any god, didn't trust myself, and never, ever trusted that things would work out. So maybe that was something I could experiment with in my thinking. It never once occurred to me to pray for anything unless I was in serious trouble: "foxhole prayers," Twelve Step program people called it. And it never occurred to me to pray for clear intuition. Not once could I remember ever living life in a relaxed state. God/religion was the barrier.

The passage also hinted at asking God for "inspiration" whenever I was stumped, unable to decide what to do, or emotionally fraught. I took that to mean listening to my intuition, which was reliably strong in me, but I'd nearly always turned away from it (again, that distrust of my instincts). Maybe I already had the beginnings of being able to do this.

Charles told me that I didn't have to adopt or rely upon a traditional, religious-based God. "You can just tune in to what feels right to you. Where do you feel calm? What makes you feel good?"

I thought about the beaches in Delaware where my family had vacationed each year. I pictured my favorite time of the year to go, the winter. No one was around, the beach was wide open and desolate, and cold wind blew sometimes gently, sometimes briskly. Gray-blue skies and crystallized sunbeams transformed the whitecaps into a magical ballet of dancing crystal lights. Closing my eyes and lying back on the bed, I pictured myself walking there, feet sinking into the cold, damp sand, wild grasses bending and flowing on the dunes in harmony with the waves.

I pictured myself shouting my failures into the wind, all the ways I'd let everyone down, let myself down, degraded myself, failed, failed, failed. I pictured my cries turning into typewriter words carried along the breeze, fluttering and expanding over the ocean and rising, rising, rising, joining the desperate words of others in the wispy strands of clouds, disappearing forever. Wrapping a blanket around my shoulders, I collapsed in the sand, so tired, emptied, and warmed by the sunlight suddenly bursting through. Closing my eyes, I fell into a long, dreamless sleep.

Waking up, I saw the room was darkening. Not quite

nighttime, but definitely no longer daytime; I figured it was near dinner. I stretched my arms and legs, pulling my back wide, long, and tight.

"Are you awake?" my roommate asked. I didn't hear her come in but was not startled by her voice.

"Yes," I answered, quietly surprised by the calm I felt.

"You were talking in your sleep," she said, a little embarrassment in her voice.

"Really? What did I say?"

"It was hard to understand, but I think you were saying things like I'm okay, I'm okay, over and over."

"Hmm. You know, I was thinking about the beach and how much I love it there."

"Oh, I love the beach," my roommate responded. "I always go to Myrtle Beach, you know, in South Carolina."

"Oh, I've been there." My voice darkened just slightly, remembering the college beach trip I'd taken with people I didn't want to remember. I shook that image off and focused on the image of Bethany Beach. "But my favorite beach is in Delaware; it's pretty empty, not much of a tourist area."

"They have beaches in Delaware?" she asked, incredulous that a place so far north from where we were could have access to sun and water.

"Yes." I giggled, thinking of how incredibly stupid this woman was. And then another thought entered quite suddenly: *She just doesn't know.* Something in me shifted, and I saw her like I'd never seen her before. Just as lost as me, looking for relief, hope, and healing. She was like a sister. She was me.

We got up and walked silently toward the cafeteria and dinner. Something inside of me felt different, and I couldn't explain it, even to myself. Puzzled, thoughts circling as I tried to analyze what I was feeling, I was stymied.

"You're really calm," my roommate remarked absent-mindedly as we stood in line to enter the dining area.

"Really?" I turned to her, questioning how she could sense that.

"Yeah. I mean, you're usually walking faster down the hall, complaining about something or other, and totally irritated about having to wait in a line. And now it's just calm; you're just calm. You don't have any of that frantic energy about you. It's nice, frankly. I don't feel like you're about to beat someone up!"

I stared at her, wide-eyed. How could she tell all that about me? "I didn't know I was so obviously irritated!" I retorted.

"Oh, you know we're all just irritated about being here. But you've changed. You are just calm. It's nice."

Schwoosh. I imagined the cold breeze of Bethany blowing through me and thought, *Yes. I do feel calm. I've let go, just for this moment.* And I knew without further explanation that everything would be all right, just as Charles and that yodeler had told me.

Part 2

mind·and·heart / [Open-mindedness]

"Until you've stopped breathing, you can always make a different choice."
—My motto

Changelings

There was a day that came when Charles the Counselor thought I was nearly ready to leave treatment. Turns out, the treatment center had been working in the background on plans for me to leave. I didn't have a place to live outside of treatment, of course. I'd defaulted and disappeared from the nasty apartment I shared in Alexandria's "condo canyon," and I was certain that my roommate there had found a suitable replacement for me, someone who could support the monthly booze budget and rent. My other alternative, which I strongly desired, was to simply pick up where I'd left off with Thomas and move into his mother's basement with him. As much as I longed for him, I knew deep down that I wouldn't stand a chance of staying clean and drink-free in that place.

I don't know how the treatment center knew I had such limited options. Since those were the days before the Healthcare Insurance Portability and Accountability Act of 1996 (HIPAA), which had strong controls over patient information and privacy, Charles the Counselor could have shared that information with the administrative staff based on information I shared in our sessions. Or perhaps it was just assumed that most people coming into treatment were coming from sketchy, unstable living situations. At any rate, Charles began talking with me about transitioning out of treatment and back into the real world, so to speak.

I was terrified. I'd been there long enough to have kicked the initial jonesing for drugs and whiskey. My body blossomed with the addition of twenty-five pounds from eating well-cooked, healthy foods. My hands began to steady, and my racking morning cough subsided. I knew my daily routine now. Wake at 7 a.m. Shower, brush my teeth, and brush out my hair. The left side, once shaved, was now growing wild spikes. Read today's morning meditation and then walk to the cafeteria for breakfast, which was a challenge in and of itself to learn how to eat. Meet for group. Take a walk, and then eat lunch. Meet with Charles and then take a long walk around the pond. (When I first arrived, I couldn't make it all the way around the pond. Now I was up to three laps around it and still had time to sit and listen to sweet guitar picking.) Return to the lecture hall for yet another lecture about the nature of addiction and how to recover. Dinner, then a Twelve Step meeting of some sort. Lights out by 10 p.m. Before I'd known it, I'd fallen into this routine and felt safe. I knew what to do and when. But the idea of managing myself outside of treatment was overwhelming, incomprehensible. There were too many choices, too many things to do. How would I know what to do and when? Most importantly, how would I not use drugs or remember not to drink alcohol?

Charles leaned forward in his chair. Then, taking my face in his hands, he leaned even closer, our foreheads nearly touching. "Karen," he said, looking deep into my eyes. He said, ever so slowly, "If you don't touch it, it won't get in you."

Mind blown. And man, did he smell good. His eyes were so deeply gray-brown and warm, and his hands held me so gently. All I wanted to do was sink into his arms.

He let go and leaned back. "So that's how that works. If you don't touch a drink, it won't get in you. You're not going to get struck drunk or high. It just won't happen. You're going to be okay."

"Are you sure?" My voice sounded like a scared five-year-old.

"Yeah. You've done great work here. You just take each day as it comes and don't worry about the rest. I know that's hard; that's the hard part. But if you just follow what you've learned here, you'll continue to be fine, and everything's going to work out. Just you wait and see. And I'll check up on you too."

He handed me my Alcoholics Anonymous book, the one Kate gave me at the airport. "Crack this open every now and then and give it a read. It'll start making more sense as time goes on."

It was months before I realized he'd signed it.

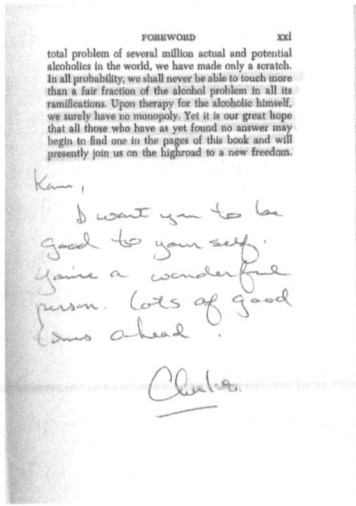

Inscription from Charles

Three weeks later, I was back in Northern Virginia. A stern but kind woman welcomed me to the halfway house she managed for badasses like myself in early recovery with nowhere else to go. I showed up with my most critical possessions in a duffel bag. The rest had been boxed up and stored in my parent's basement, including my most prized and favored things: my books and vinyl record collection. It would be more than a year before I saw them again.

The home had free parking for residents, a strict routine, mandatory Twelve Step meeting attendance, and an extensive chore list. No men were allowed in, and all bedroom doors were required to stay open at all times, even during sleeping hours. Not a shred of privacy. A heated outrage brewed inside me.

"I can't stand vacuuming," I protested, having been assigned that chore my first day.

"Too bad," the headmistress replied. "You could try swapping chores with someone, but eventually, you'll rotate through each duty. You may as well suck it up and get the work done."

AAARRGGGHHHH. Stifling any response, I vacuumed the living room and stairs as quickly and as noisily as I could, huffing my complaints, making it clear that speed and not quality was my goal.

Waking up, panic gripped my throat. I rolled over and lit a cigarette before fully opening my eyes. Taking a long drag, my throat choked, and I broke into a hacking coughing fit. My body was more awake, and I looked around. White walls, nothing on them. Boring. A single window, dull light filtering in through simple, sheer white curtains. Underneath stood a simple wood desk with a small single-shelf hutch upon which I'd stacked my recovery books. The chair had seen better days. In the closet hung a wardrobe that lasted about five days before being fully rotated. A round ombré-brown braided-rope rug in the center of the room offered no warmth and little cheer. And, of course, an opened door through which the morning breakfast scent entered: black coffee, blueberry muffins, bacon, and cheesy eggs.

My morning panic set in, and I couldn't remember what to do first. My mind raced through possible options.

Option 1
- Get dressed
- Wash my face and brush my teeth
- Read today's meditation
- Go down for breakfast

Option 2
- Before getting dressed, wash my face and brush my teeth
- Read today's meditation
- Get dressed
- Go down for breakfast

Option 3
- Read today's meditation
- Get dressed
- Go down for breakfast
- Wash my face and brush my teeth after eating

Aaagghhhhhhhhhh. Too many choices, and I didn't want to make a mistake. You have to set the tone right from the start to have a good, productive day! I sat on my bed, frozen in terrified indecision. Bolting up like a fire being lit under my ass, I ran in my pajamas to the pay phone down the hall and dialed the only person I knew would tell me what the right answer was: my new sponsor.

My sponsor was a woman I'd met the first night I came home from treatment. It was a Saturday night, during which our curfew at the home was extended two full hours, allowing me to attend a dance at a local recovery club. Having been used to going out dancing at Poseur's every night in my earlier life, I couldn't wait to go to a club dance. In my mind, it was a promise of young people, people my age, hip and cool people like me who couldn't stand not drinking and not getting messed up and who were desperate to connect, laugh, and have wild, raucous sex pushed up against bathroom walls with total strangers. My idea of a great night.

The reality was disappointingly, horribly, devastatingly different. Tucked away behind and above Brown's Hardware Store in an old, drab, brown brick suburban strip mall, the club desperately needed fresh paint. Dingy, smoke-stained, greenish-yellow walls opened to one large smoke-filled room where an off-key and offbeat band of a few people in early recovery badly attempted a few cover songs from the seventies. The tambourine player walked on and off at random times. It was questionable how long they had played together or if they'd even practiced before that night.

The mostly middle-aged dance attendees lined the walls. No one was on the dance floor. People milled about, talking in small groups, and several stood awkwardly alone. Stunned, I turned and stormed down the fifteen steps to the outside parking lot. Finding a stoop to sit on, I bummed a cigarette from another dance victim sitting next to me, fired it up, and sucked in a big drag. Heart pounding from disappointment and anger, I felt I'd been lied to. A sucker.

A woman I hadn't noticed turned to me. "What's the matter, honey? You not having any fun?"

"No," I choked out. "This fucking sucks. I can't believe this is my life now." My cheeks flushed, and a wave of heat spiked up my throat and jaw and threatened to unleash the tears I fought back.

"Oh, honey. If you're not having fun, you're not doing this right! Why don't you come with me? I'll teach you how to have fun!"

I looked at her more closely. She was beautiful, with long, straight brown hair, big, round, twinkly eyes, and a gorgeous smile. Maybe five years older than me.

"Really? What time is it?" I asked.

"Oh, I'll get you where you need to be on time. Don't worry. Let's go have coffee."

She was hell-bent on me learning how to have fun in a sober state, which sounded completely implausible, a poor imitation of what life should be like, especially for someone in their twenties.

"Oh honey, you have no idea what's in front of you! It's gonna be great, trust me. The first thing you should do is pick up service work—you know, help another alcoholic or addict. That'll get you out of yourself, and you'll start to feel better."

That got me thinking. After gaining what can only be described as a rapid accumulation of points charged against my license due to a spate of speeding tickets, I lost my driver's license for a year. Yet I continued to drive. There weren't many convenient public transportation options in Washington, DC, at least none I was comfortable using. I figured if I just drove carefully, if I didn't get into an accident or have any cause to be pulled over, no one would know my license was suspended.

I was lonely, having left Thomas, and I didn't know any young guys who were sober—except a slew of them at The Salvation Army. *I bet they need rides to meetings*, I thought. I'd heard about people giving other people rides to meetings as a form of "fellowship" and "service." Plus, I secretly hoped I'd meet someone I could at least hook up with since it was strongly suggested that I avoid getting into a relationship the first year I was trying to be sober.

After a few weeks of solid service work, I told my sponsor how proud I was that I was actually doing what she suggested.

"I can't believe how willing I am to follow through with your suggestions." I beamed at her at lunch over our salads.

"So let me get this straight. You're driving your car and transporting guys from The Salvation Army to meetings? Isn't your license suspended?"

"Well, technically, it is, but I'm being really careful."

She laughed. "Well, honey, I think it's great that you're taking suggestions from me and being willing, but sweetie, if you get caught driving on a suspended license, you're going to jail." She waited as my thoughts caught up. "I mean, honey, there's a lot of other ways to be of service."

"Are you kidding me? I could go to jail?"

"Oh yeah. They won't bat an eye at that if you get caught. And you know, now that you're in recovery, you have so many more options. You don't have to put yourself at risk. You don't need to live in ways that keep you afraid of getting caught doing something. Why don't you consider parking that car over at your parents' until you get your license back, and we can look for other ways to be of service?"

I had dreaded this moment. I'd always had a car, always

had freedom and control, could come and go as I wanted, ever since I had been able to drive. It was a hard, hard concession, but I knew she was right. I needed to surrender to reality.

We left her car at the diner and picked up another program friend, who followed us. My sponsor drove while I sat miserably in the passenger seat, feeling sorry for myself and furious that it would be another year before I would be able to get my car back. We dropped my car at my parents' home, got in the return car, and went to a meeting where I signed on to be a greeter.

Letting go of the car and reconciling myself to the consequences of my former life choices knocked my innate arrogance down a few pegs. It also forced me to start asking for rides to meetings. Despite all my resistance, I started meeting more people, and my world opened up in a way I hadn't imagined. The first inklings of gratitude tingled my spirit, and I soon found myself smiling more, relaxing a little more, and feeling more assured that things would work themselves out. Steps one, two, and three were coming alive in my life.

As a condition of returning to work, the Academy arranged for me to have weekly sessions with a psychiatrist located within walking distance of the office. Dr. Q was an older, balding, vest-wearing, round-bellied man. Thoughtful, he stood when I entered his office for my first session. "Sit down," he kindly said, pointing to the chair in front of his very prestigious walnut desk.

Leaning back in his chair, he stroked his chin and said, "You're late, which indicates a natural disregard for other people. You're also disrespectful, which naturally is part and parcel of being late to appointments. That also tends to be indicative of generalized laziness, possible stupidity, and clear shortsightedness. There's no doubt you are entitled, demanding, wildly moody, and selfish." He continued on this track for at least five minutes while I sat, waiting.

He sat up sharply.

"You know you don't need to listen to this, right?"

Wait. *What*? My head tilted like a dog.

"Someone in your life primed you for taking abuse. You would just sit and politely listen to this, and worse if I just continued, am I right?"

I nodded.

"You don't need to listen to this. You could get up and leave. You could stop me. You could get angry. You could argue back. Someone did this to you, and this is where our work will begin. You don't deserve to be treated like this, and you need to understand that this isn't what you are here for. Are you ready to begin?"

Therapy with Dr. Q wasn't nearly as enjoyable as counseling had been with Charles. To begin with, Dr. Q was a lot older than Charles. His look was a blend of Alfred Hitchcock and a 1950s school principal. He offered nearly nothing, usually asked me a single question, then leaned back in his chair, round glasses scooching down his nose, a barely concealed bemused look crossing his face, glancing down and taking notes.

His questions weren't easy. Each session began with a softball to loosen me up, usually something like "How are you feeling today?" Believe it or not, that was a challenge to figure out most days. Pissed off? Craving anything mind-altering?

Frustrated? All of the above, most days. He would lean back, pause, and ask, "Is that all?" It wasn't long before I realized I didn't have the vocabulary to articulate my feelings.

"You're 'pissed off.' That's what you said. What does that mean, exactly?"

I thought hard about this.

"Well, I can't drive, which is a pain. And it isn't fair—it's not like I got a DWI or something. My roommate has a kitten that she won't get fixed, and it bleeds all over my room, which is disgusting. I keep telling her to keep the damn cat out of my stuff, but she won't listen to me. No one listens to me! It's just so hard. No one likes me." I choked back sudden tears, shocked by their uninvited, threatening eruption.

"You're lonely."

Boom. There it was. Yes. A word to add to my vernacular.

"So, this 'pissed off' feeling is really anger, which you prefer over feeling sad and lonely."

Oh, great. We get to add sad to the mix too. A little heat flashed up my throat and cheeks.

"Well, of course I'm lonely. I was *forced* to give up my boyfriend, my club, my friends." Tears ignored my command to stay put, and they fell, one by one, onto my clenched hand.

"You're a victim."

"Well, yes. When you put it like that, yes. I've taken so much crap from people—"

My voice gave out. I looked at him, and there he was, leaning back like a fat scholarly Buddha, round belly right at my sight line as his amused smile shamelessly shone on his face.

"You know you can make different choices. You aren't a victim at all, really, are you? You just want the easy way out: to blame everyone else."

"Oh, okay, so if you're so smart, what other choices can I

make? I mean, the damn roommate won't do anything about the damn cat . . ."

"Does your door lock? You could lock your door when you aren't in your room."

Well, yes. I could do that, but wouldn't that seem weird?
"Okay. I'll try that."

"You could look for another place to live."

Yes. I guess I could. I just hate moving, especially since I'm not the one with the stupid cat making a mess everywhere.

"You could also check to see how close you are to getting your license back and exactly what you need to do to get it back."

"Yeah, I could. I mean, I *think* I know all that, but I'm not exactly sure. So this is like 'footwork,' what my sponsor tells me I have to do. She says all I have to do is the footwork, and the results will fall into place."

"Your sponsor sounds like a wise adviser. I would listen to her."

The session ended, and weirdly, I felt peaceful.

Another word to add to my list.

―――

Even though it would be another six months before I could reclaim my driver's license, my sober roommates booted me from the sober house, and I was fired from my job on the same day. I had stayed clean and alcohol-free, but I refused to make any other changes (*it wasn't me, right? It was the alcohol and the drugs.*) But without doing the deeper work, I stayed that same arrogant, nasty, foulmouthed, lonely, violent, terrified girl who dropped her bags in treatment. In desperation, I ran to a pay phone, dialed my sponsor, and shouted, "I THOUGHT THINGS WOULD GET BETTER.

WHY AREN'T THEY BETTER?"

She laughed and asked a simple question: "Are you ready to do the work? Feelings follow action. Not the other way around."

I surrendered. Again. Completely. Depressed, despite believing my life would never be fun, filled with laughter or adventure, I opened my mind as best as I could and listened. Without any sense of a relationship with a higher power, much less a god, I wrote in my journal all the things I had failed at, all the things I had done, and a few things that I could honestly say I did somewhat well (at my sponsor's insistence). Before I knew it, Step Four was done. Then I haltingly told that gnarly truth to a trusted person and had an experience that many in the program shared after completing Step Five. For the first time, I no longer felt alone. That glass wall I'd always felt I walked behind shattered, and I felt okay in ways the drugs and alcohol could not entirely fix. For the first time, I experienced being accepted and even celebrated by someone despite all the horribleness about myself I'd just shared. But I still had strong compulsions to drink and use that would hit me out of nowhere.

Embracing a one-day-at-a-time approach touted by the Twelve Step elders, I promised myself each day that I could get obliterated the following day if I really couldn't stand being straight and sober anymore. Meetings offered a daily refuge. Without even realizing it, though, that strong compulsion to use lifted slowly. Another year passed. My senses improved: colors became brilliant, and music was mesmerizing. I fell in love with humans and sunlight and energy. Hope trotted alongside the shame I still felt, and I dared to think about new possibilities.

Healing happened slowly. Intentionally, at times, and on levels beyond my awareness. As my mind opened, my curiosity expanded. Crystal healing, yoga, Jungian therapy, reiki, cognitive behavioral therapy, visualization, art, Tarot, and mental health medication came together in a blend of modalities. I became a certified transformational breathwork healer. There was little I wouldn't learn about, get curious about, and experiment with.

The IBM Selectric typewriter at my work desk was revolutionized to one that could hold two lines of text in memory.

Two years clean and sober, and I flirted with perfection. I quit smoking, sugar, sex, television, and anything that wasn't organic. Having stabilized enough to live on my own, I curated a home-decorating scheme, complete with a comfortable color palette for the walls and a mix of thrift store finds and new furnishings to make my new condo a home. I exercised, swam a mile every other day, and cycled the four miles daily to a publishing job I had always wanted. Yet I found myself wound so tight, confused again, questioning why I had so much outward success but remained feeling lost and empty inside. I couldn't feel again; I returned to a floating sensation above my life, viewing it from behind a light panel of glass. Numb. Shame beckoned again, slipped under my door, slid across the hardwood floors, under the covers, and into my heart. While I had been faithfully abstinent from all mood-altering drugs and alcohol, had I failed to recover? Was I stuck forever in this purgatory of not being fully here but unable to leave? That old familiar thought that there was something deeply wrong with me drummed steadily in my head, and I felt I was losing my mind. Nothing I was doing worked, and I knew I needed to change.

Yogaville and the Lotus Shrine

God wasn't a concept I had gotten any more comfortable with. I mean, it brings up all kinds of things, doesn't it? Wars started in the name of God. Injustice, corruption, all the things. Priests abusing kids. I didn't want any part of it.

But I was intrigued to hear that there's a difference between religion and God. I just didn't know how to access spirituality without a religion, without someone telling me where to go, what to do, and how to pray.

"Go to a bookstore and let a book find you," my sponsor directed.

What does that even mean? I thought. But I felt so hollow and lost, I was willing to try it. Plus, I loved bookstores and the best one (in my opinion), an absolute institution to the written word and the lifestyles around writing, was Kramers books.

I loved everything about that place. Smack in the center of Dupont Circle in DC, it had everything: a wide-ranging selection of books, a fantastic kitchen, and a vibe perfect for meandering exploration. Timeless.

Wandering through the store, a low volume of Rare Essence playing overhead, the sweet smell of freshly baked bread wafting through, I felt I could stay forever. *This is my happy place*, I thought, catching myself smiling as I passed a small oval mirror at the end of an aisle. Slowly bypassing new releases, bestsellers, fiction, sci-fi, nonfiction, and education, I turned right into the self-help aisle.

A balding man with kind eyes and a fluffy white beard caught my eye. His three-quarter-face photo sought a connection with someplace high above, caught in the cover of a book. An unfamiliar warmth softly spread in my chest, and I moved past him. I paused and took three steps back. Picking up the book, I read the back cover:

"By nature, the mind and body are happy and healthy, peaceful and restful."
—Sri Swami Satchidananda

Turning quickly away, I walked to the end of the aisle and briskly walked back to the front of the store, scanning the new releases. Stephen King's *It* tempted me. I considered the book for a moment when a thought thundered in my head: *If you want to be truly happy, pay attention to what you consume.*

Turning and leaning against the wall, I thought about what I consumed by listening, reading, watching, or eating: Stephen King (I was an avid fan), the nightly news, work stress, fast food, family arguments, and my friends' problems.

It dawned on me that as long as I consumed stressful things, I would be anything but happy, healthy, peaceful, and restful.

Right there, I decided to parent my mind. I'd change what I focused on and, as an experiment, would cut out anything stressful from my daily "consumption" for a year to see what would happen. After all, I didn't have much to lose. I was already in a constant state of stress. Whenever I parked in Alexandria, Arlington, or DC, my car was ticketed, booted, or towed from years of unpaid parking tickets. I felt tired, moody, cranky, and irritated most days. Work was hard and stressful. Maybe, just maybe, the stress I was feeling had something to do with what I was focusing on each day.

A quiet excitement filled me. I whispered goodbye to Mr. King and returned to the self-help aisle. It was the only book I saw, as if a spotlight lit up its spot on the shelf. I picked up *To Know Your Self: The Essential Teachings of Swami Satchidananda*, paid the clerk at the cashier, and began a journey of spiritual awakening that would carry me forward for decades through loves and losses, moves and adventures, vocations and careers, and for evolutions that continue today.

I turned off the TV for thirty days. When I turned it back on, the power sparked, there was a loud POOF, and a single round pinpoint of light appeared on the screen, leaving a split second later. The screen settled into black. "The TV died," I yelled out to no one.

With nothing left to distract me, I curled up on the couch and picked up the book that had found me. I'd excitedly bought it over a month ago, reported to my sponsor that a book had indeed "found" me, and promptly put it down, unopened. I had a habit of always reading the last page first of a book, so that's where I began. Turning the book over, the lower left corner of the back cover caught my eye: Integral Yoga Publications, Yogaville, Virginia. Stunned, I realized that the publisher was in my home state. I was eager to find this Yogaville and visit it.

Years before the emergence of the internet as we know it today, research in the 1980s was more like hands-on sleuthing. I started by visiting the Alexandria library and asking a librarian how to find out about a town called Yogaville. She sent me in the direction of geography and maps. A quick search in the card catalog for Yogaville, Virginia, yielded the Integral Yoga Magazine series. Pulling the most recent copy from the Periodicals section and turning to the masthead revealed the mailing address: 1 Yogaville Way, Buckingham, Virginia. Buckingham! Now I had a town to search for.

Thoroughly gripped with my mission to find this elusive place, I searched for maps of Virginia. I felt like a modern-day Nancy Drew. I located the Rand McNally map section and opened a roadmap of Virginia. Breath held, I searched the index for Buckingham. I turned to page four, running my fingers down the grid to C4, landing nearly smack in the state's middle. Just above the town of Buckingham was a winding elbow of the James River, making it the perfect place for the Yogaville ashram and the Light of the Universal Truth Shrine (LOTUS).

I knew I had to go.

A week later, I had a bag packed and began a pilgrimage of 166 miles to the place that would become my spiritual retreat center, a place where I could begin a journey toward opening my heart. A place where I began the experience of knowing a sense of God and the Universe, within me, within you, and all around all of us, all the time. It was the first place where I explored the idea of creating a relationship with the spiritual realm outside of an organized church, and it was where I learned that the journey was about the human physical experience too. The body and this place on earth had never been comfortable for me. Remember, I'd endured so much suffering and so much that I had not even acknowledged. I only knew that I never felt safe, had never felt "in" my body; I existed as if behind that pane of glass, always watching, listening for all that went on around me, never a part of it. I was always a bit removed, distanced, detached. Yogaville was the first place where I learned that the suffering I'd felt had a name, and I wasn't alone in what I was feeling or experiencing.

Arriving at the ashram, I was greeted by a small family of white-tailed deer grazing in the green strips of the parking lot. I entered the registration area, where I was warmly welcomed.

"Namaste. Welcome," the yogi greeted me. "What brings you to Yogaville today?"

"I don't know, actually," I answered. "I just learned about this place and thought since I lived in Virginia, I should visit. I think I'm here to learn something, but I don't know exactly what."

"It sounds like you've been brought here on a personal transformation journey," the yogi offered.

"Yes! I think that sounds right."

"Why don't we arrange for you to begin with a personal retreat? How long can you stay?"

"Well, I could stay the weekend, I think. How much does it cost, and what's included?"

"We suggest a donation that is quite affordable for you. There are three vegan meals offered each day, time for meditation, several hatha yoga classes, and opportunities for Karma yoga, which is service. You can also arrange to meet with a swami for spiritual guidance, if you would like."

I couldn't believe it. *Find a book*, my sponsor had told me. It was as if a door to a magical kingdom was opening before me, and a welcome carpet custom-made for me was being laid at my feet.

"Yes. Thank you. I'm so glad I'm here," I said, and a new warmth sparked in my chest, inviting my shoulders to relax. *That must be a good sign*, I thought. *I don't know what's happening, but then again, I don't need to know right now.* I followed the yogi into Sivananda Hall and a new world of spirituality.

*Photo courtesy of Bill Geoghegan,
©2023 Satchidananda Ashram—Yogaville*

The Lotus Shrine, or Light of Truth Universal Shrine, holds chapels for each major world's religions. There were many I'd never heard of. After joining the sunrise meditation sessions, I was changed. Inevitably, all of God's word, all permutations of a higher power, all paths lead to the same place. Our egos, so desperately attached to having some meaning in this life, of being someone, something, find snippets of our family myths, generational traumas, and truths, portions of the stories we tell ourselves, the choices that we make, and the outcomes. From that isolated and closely curated stew, we create an identity to which we become particularly attached. That's where our ego feels seen and known and that we as individuals matter. And so, our sense of a higher power—if we have one at all, if it was given as part of our family journey, something we adopted ourselves into later in life, or something we created—provides language, culture, stories, myths, wisdom, ceremony, and names that align to our own identity. It feels accessible and relatable, and it becomes a place of comfort.

A week later, I was still at the ashram. It took three full days for my mind to quiet from the low-grade despair, shame, and constant chatter of what I thought I was supposed to be doing and who I thought I was supposed to be that lurked in the background of my existence. Anxiety. A hint of space opened, and I could hear the swami's mantra in my ear: Om Shanti Om. Om Shanti Shanti Shanti. Om, a sacred word, a sacred sound. Shanti, peace. Taken together, it's a grounding sound, vibrating deep in my chest wall, hijacking my vagus nerve, and pulsing waves of peace throughout my enteric nervous system. For the first time, I truly felt my gut. I could breathe, deeply breathe without effort. A new energy was moving in me: a quiet, low-key anticipation of things to come. I felt at peace. I felt renewed.

Returning

I wanted to feel better about myself. There was an inner fear that I was rotten from the inside out, that there was something inherently wrong with me, and nothing I tried could make that better. The more I tried to do better, be a better person, a better worker, a better friend, a better family member, the more I failed, and my failings were so obvious. It was years before I understood that I'd always felt that way about myself and that it started with my relationship with my mother. I had always assumed I'd done something to piss her off, something so unforgivable that it would make sense why she treated me the way she did. I used to explain it to friends, laughing to make light of it, to make it seem like I'd just handled it, that it wasn't killing me the way it truly was, that when I was born, we sort of looked at each other and said, *Naw*, turning away from each other. That's how it seemed, and it seemed the only thing that could explain the nature of our relationship. The wound I felt inside was grief for the absence of the mother I wanted—a mother wound. As my recovery continued, I came to recognize that the origin of this grief lived within me. While I had been a child, I continuously compared myself and my relationship with my mother to others, which seemed idyllic. With a child's mind and emotional development, I was consumed with what I wanted and what I seemed to lack.

As I learned to deepen my inner examination and exploration through the Twelve Steps and therapy, I learned that I was the one who had failed to see and accept my mother exactly as she was. She was the mother I was given; she was part of who shaped me and stewarded the first significant journey in my spiritual development. She saw my self-obsession with my feelings and my emotional state. She saw my escapism in alcohol, drugs, and the lifestyle that came with it. She did not flinch from the truth and did not believe in enabling me. She stood with a high degree of strength and integrity. Her demeanor with me was an expression not of rejection but born from a fierce protective force. My mother was never a cuddly bear; she was the alpha lioness of our family.

My childish mind could not see that, though. I longed for the mothers I saw on TV and assumed my friends had: those who did their nails, played, and whispered girly secrets to each other. In time, and with more recovery, the blame I used to box in my mother eased into a sense of curiosity. I wanted to know who she was and what her path had been. It took years for us to develop trust, for us to be able to sit down and have actual conversations. I learned that she had suffered in terrible, terrible ways as a child. Rheumatic fever at age five threatened her life and left her with a heart murmur and debilitating arthritis. The loss of her mother through awful years of cancer slowly and methodically devoured her. And then, in her teens, after her mother's death, assuming responsibility for her younger sister and the household at large while her father was hospitalized for a broken back, a result of a coal-mining accident, well, her life had not been easy. I don't know if I would have survived it. As the years continued, I saw parts of her that I had previously refused to acknowledge or not even seen: her wicked, sassy humor, her silliness, her razor-sharp mind, her brilliant common sense. The judgment I had, I realized, was a direct result of how I judged her and myself. I was the one who had been unfair.

My newfound appreciation of my mother did not erase history or negate things that had happened to me in my childhood. She was responsible for her behavior and her choices. But as she is responsible for her actions, I'm responsible for my attitudes, perspectives, actions, forgiveness, and acceptance. Through spiritual work, this miraculous restoration of our relationship bloomed. Today, we talk, laugh, share stories, celebrate wins and dreams, shop, share meals, and make memories. I'm so grateful we could get to this place where we enjoy each other's company while she's still alive.

I realized that learning about spirituality and the differences it can have with organized religion can deeply alter the relationships I have with myself and others. I saw that as my journey with my mother changed. I tried meditation. My path inward began with the study of mindfulness with the writings of Thich Nhat Hanh. I devoured recordings of his walking meditations because I could not sit still. Meditation with busy hands was another way in, and I found myself realizing how quiet my mind was and how time flew when I was washing dishes at my kitchen sink, staring out of the window, watching the seasons change through the color of the leaves of the cherry tree centered in the window frame.

An IBM PC XT replaced my IBM Selectric typewriter.

Webmail replaced phone calls and message pads. Novell networks connected everything at work, ushering in the "sitting is the new smoking" age since you didn't have to get up to walk anywhere anymore. My job at the magazine ended. In desperation, I moved to Columbia, Maryland, with a new boyfriend, despite the roller-coaster nature of our relationship. He was so smart; he was the computer guy from *The Baltimore Sun* I called when my computer or network didn't work. He later confessed that he intentionally didn't fix my computer the first time he came on-site so I'd call him again and he'd have to come back. He was looking for a way to ask me out. We ended up dating long distance; he from just outside of Baltimore and me from my little condo in Alexandria, a lovely white brick one-bedroom home with a garden I built in the backyard. We mostly saw each other on weekends. Steve would drive down, exhausted, weaving in rush-hour traffic through two cities, and I would be so anxious to see him. He would be cranky, resentful that he couldn't smoke pot at my home to unwind, and therefore edgy all weekend. I never went to his house. Eventually, when I left the magazine with a new job in Columbia, Maryland, we decided to move in together and rent a home there.

It didn't go well. It promised to start off well enough, but before long, he was spending more time away from home. His normally quiet, soft voice grew a brassy edge. "This is my home too, you know." He would open his argument in a tone both pleading and irate. "I don't have a problem with pot, and it's unfair that I can't smoke in my own home."

"Well, it's illegal," I'd counter (in 1987). "And there are healthier ways to relax," I'd offer.

It wasn't long before he stopped arguing and stayed out later. As he found his weekend happiness on the tennis courts, finding his next love in his mixed doubles partner,

I retreated further into myself. *What is wrong with me?* I would whisper in our bed, alone in the dark.

Feeling desperate, I reached for my journal. "What depression is like," I began.

I am in a depression. I finally sought help tonight. My sponsor, she understands. What relief that word brings. She knows. She could tell me the things I'm afraid to say.

What it's like . . .

I can't sleep . . . and then I sleep forever. Dirty clothes, dirty dishes, all of them. Desperate, I feel desperate all the time, and I try so hard to tell people all the neat things I do (the little things, the basic things, cooking . . .) a major accomplishment.

Desperate because I'm falling apart.

I'm so sad. And. I can't hide it tonight.

Fighting suicide all the time

Scared—all the time, afraid to leave my house, I'm not even going to work tomorrow. I don't see how I can. It's 3:15 in the morning. I'll oversleep.

I can't hold on much longer. And I tell myself SNAP OUT OF IT! Goddamn it! Stop feeling SORRY FOR YOURSELF! Go to a meeting! I hate them, the meetings.

My sponsor said, "Go to someone and let them pamper you."

Who?

I needed an escape route out of that roller-coaster relationship and found it in a government contract that included relocation to Harford County, Maryland. I would be an on-site office manager at an army base near the top of the Chesapeake Bay. Established in October 1917, about six months after the United States entered World War I, the government built federally-owned plants to manufacture and test toxic gasses. The manufacturing area became the army's arsenal, which manufactured mustard gas, nitro chloroform, and phosgene. It also built separate facilities to arm artillery shells with those chemicals. From its inception to the present day, the base ran chemical research programs, including human testing on the effect and impact of chemical warfare agents, protective clothing, and pharmaceuticals.

Arriving in a nearby town to look at rentals a week before my job started, I stopped at a convenience store to get a soda, looked up, and saw a sign that summed up this new culture: BEL AIR GUN PAWN LIQUOR.

There was a dusty man in ragged jeans, a ten-gallon hat low over his brown, leaning over, cupped hands, his back to the wind as he smoked, standing at the side of the store. *Where the hell have I landed?* I thought.

A week later, I was unceremoniously moved out of Steve's life and back fully into my own as a nearing-thirty single woman in an unfamiliar world at the top of the Chesapeake Bay. Having always romanticized country life as warm, cozy, welcoming, and simple, I looked forward to this new beginning, maybe meeting a cowboy or two and finding that elusive peace and balance I'd sought. I was excited about embracing my new role as an office manager, which I was certain would finally propel me out of the stagnant, blocked, unremarkable destiny I feared as a glorified typist, which, because I was a young woman without a college degree, was the box in which I'd been placed by default, no matter how earnestly I tried to escape it.

Reality set in quickly. We were delayed from installing the double-wide trailers that would serve as our "office" for the duration of the contract. Each time the army did a ground scan, they hit multiple unexploded ordinances on the site. In other words, no one could even walk over that parking lot space because there were live bombs buried for lack of an alternate, proper disposal. Removals and re-scans continued until all the bombs were removed and the ground was considered safe. I was inexperienced, ill-equipped, and uninformed in my role, so another man on the contract took control of the contract, the office management, and the site. I was infuriated. After the trailers were installed, equipped, and furnished, we began our daily routines, reporting to work at the site. Tony sat in front of me. He was a noisy chewer, a loud talker on the phone, and generally patronizing and dismissive. To help me manage my hot resentment, I built a wall of books at the edge of my desk, blocking my view of him.

One afternoon, Tony stood at my left shoulder as I sat at my station. "Copy these for me," he said, dropping a binder of factory blueprints and specs on my desk. He took a step back and waited.

"I'm sorry. I'm busy right now," I mumbled.

"Did you not hear me?" Tony asked. I could just picture the rise of his left eyebrow.

"Okay." I quickly stood, grabbed the binder, and walked the ten steps to the copy machine, conscious that he followed close behind me.

I lifted the copier lid and opened the binder, readying the page flat against the glass screen.

"Not like that!" Tony grabbed my right arm, firm, above the elbow and whipped me around. Pinning me against the trailer wall, he moved close to my face. I could see every large acne pus-filled pore on his face, his too-narrow eyes squinting under busy brown brows.

"Get off me!" I squirmed and pushed him back. Startled, he lost his grip and staggered a step or two back. I stormed out of the trailer and saw the chief chemist smoking. "Can I bum one of those?" I asked, hands and voice shaking.

"Sure. Are you okay?"

"No. That freaking asshole Tony just put his hands on me."

"Oh, wow, that's not okay. What are you going to do about it?"

I took a deep drag off the cigarette, instantly blowing a year of not smoking, and a rush of adrenaline flooded my system, calming me down. "I'm not sure yet, but you better believe he's messed with the wrong person."

Going home, I considered my options. Here I was, living alone in Riverside, Maryland, with my neighbor's goats chewing the siding on my rented townhouse. Jobs were scarce here, especially high-paying ones. It was all farming, baseball, and the US Army. And in this instance, Tony and the whole management team were in the wrong. They'd gotten comfortable slapping women's backsides in the office. Catcalls were common, as were dirty jokes at our expense. That was just wrong, especially on a federal facility. The worst part was how complicit the Army commanders and upper management were. They blatantly turned a blind eye every time a complaint was registered or they were in the room when a conduct violation occurred. Not only did they not stop the behavior, but they chuckled or smiled creepily.

I thought about what Dr. Q had said to me during my first session with him. *I'm not here to take abuse.* I considered the other women on the government contract who were also subjected to the treatment I'd experienced. I considered what I had learned from moving in with Steve despite knowing it wouldn't work out and willingly giving up a home and area that I loved to maintain a fantasy of something I thought I wanted. *What did that cost me?* I considered whether I wanted to keep living that way or push what I knew was right for me down, way, way down, and what that took now that I wasn't able to use alcohol or drugs to stifle the voice inside me that screamed over and over how much more I wanted for myself. I considered what I was best at. I considered what I thought would be possible if I took a leap of faith.

So, I wrote a letter to the company's grievance officer detailing all I had experienced and witnessed over the past eleven months on the contract, citing all the employment laws I could find that could possibly support my allegations. The response was swift and definitive: in exchange for agreeing not to sue the company or the US Army or disclose the nature of my severance, the company would provide me the opportunity to resign with the possibility of rehiring, pack my home, and offer full relocation to a destination of my choice. If I decided not to move, they would offer me comparable compensation.

I took the money.

Months later, I married a man simply because he asked and because I thought it was time. Walking down the aisle in what had become the wedding my mother always wanted, I knew I was making a dreadful mistake. Everything in me wanted to run. It was as if a portal to the underworld beckoned me at the end of that aisle, my new moments-away-from-being-my-husband man morphing into Hades himself. Panicked, I looked to the sky to open up, wishing a descending dragon would swallow me whole. Instead, my father tearfully kissed me away to the next level of lessons destined for me, and this time, what was at stake was my very life itself.

First-time bride

Miracles

Waking up under a gray sky, low thunder rumbling in the distance, I felt alone and realized my husband was gone. *Off to work*, I guessed, and I absently rubbed the hard, dry corner of the cuticle on my left thumb. I bit it off, too hard and too deep, an ooze of dark red blood slowly filling the base of the nail.

I felt gross. In complete confusion over who this person was that I'd married, I realized there was nothing here in this marriage, my work, or in Maryland. Still clean and sober, I recognized that familiar emptiness inside. Whenever I felt anything, it was usually in the form of nausea. *What have I done with my life?* I bitterly thought. It's like I didn't care anymore, like I had been sleepwalking into this situation and couldn't find a way out.

It seemed ridiculous to get divorced after only being married a few months. But honestly, the day we came home from a short honeymoon in Maine, it was like a switch flipped inside my husband. Even though I commuted an hour each way to work, he came home after his local job and demanded—no, commanded in a threatening voice—that dinner should have been done, the table properly set, and the laundry put away. And he had moved into my home!

The nights were getting weirder and creepier. I waited until the mornings after he'd left for work, risking my job by delaying my arrival, and secretly called my sponsor for advice.

"He's big into watching porn with me, which is pretty disgusting and not at all a turn-on. He wants me to act out what he's watching on the TV while he's watching it. I mean, Lord knows I'm no virgin, but this is seriously grossing me out."

"He's using you, Karen. It doesn't sound like he's in any way in touch with the fact that you are his wife, a woman, and deserve to be treated well, even behind closed doors. Have you talked to him about this?"

"I've tried, but he just either blows me off or gets angry and says I'm not doing my part of upholding my marriage vows. It's weird. It's like he turned into a completely different person. I don't know what to do."

"It's okay to say you made a mistake and don't want this marriage. Have you thought about getting it annulled? Or at least separate to think about what you really want?"

The thought of separating also made me sick. The money my parents had poured into this wedding was enormous. My mother couldn't stand my husband or his family but decided that if I were going to go through with marrying this guy, she would show them who we were. She would produce the most tasteful upstaged event she could muster, and pockets were deep. How could I admit that this was all for naught, a waste of money, time, and dreams, especially after disappointing them and her for most of my life?

When I told my parents I was getting married, it was as if I opened the door to my mother's dreams and floated into her event-planning power. As graciously as I could, I acquiesced to anything and everything she wanted, even the gown she decided I should wear, the colors, the handmade bridesmaids' gowns, the vendors, the food, and the guest list.

In a seemingly numbed state, I dreamily drifted along with her excitement, vision, and will. All that seemed to matter to me was that I absolutely did not disappoint her.

I knew I had entered the marriage in a numb, passive state. My only desire was to avoid conflict and make my husband happy, but I quickly realized what that would cost. It finally came down to a choice between living and dying. I had to wake up and own myself, my spirit, and my destiny.

One Sunday evening, as I was finishing the dishes and getting organized for the workweek, he walked in from a day out of the house. Stomping the mud off his shoes, he didn't say a word, but instead he walked through the living room, glowering in my direction as he stopped in front of the kitchen doorway.

"So, you didn't wait for me to eat? What in the hell am I supposed to eat for dinner?" he growled, a red flush lighting up his cheeks. I saw that his hands were clenched.

"I'm sorry! I didn't know when you would be home. I can fix you something. What would you like?"

He harrumphed. "You are so useless. It's too late! I'm just going to bed. I'm stressed and exhausted. No thanks to you."

I finished getting ready for the next day and joined him upstairs. The tension had been palpable for so long, and I worried that if we didn't talk things through, the tight lid that kept the problems, anger, and frustration down would burst, and something terrible would happen. Taking a deep breath, I stood in the bedroom doorway. He was sitting up in bed, glaring once in my direction, and then ignored me, turning his attention to the TV, the sound turned down.

Softening and lowering the pitch of my voice, I said, "I know it's late and you're tired and obviously upset. I don't want to hash anything out right now, but I wanted to let you know that I think we should talk soon, sometime this week, you know, about the issues in our marriage."

I paused.

Slowly turning his head toward me, his throat thick with anger, and he shouted, "What fucking issues? What issues?"

My heart jumped into my throat and beat hard. As calmly as I could, I responded, "Well, for example, how you are talking to me right now is unacceptable, and I think you've been trying to get me to accept unacceptable behavior." Terrified of an explosion and panicked that I'd get hurt, I took two steps back as he roared, jumping out of bed, his glare never leaving my eyes. He was shaking.

I shook as I stood my ground, knees shaking, hands shaking. He strode over to me, completely red in his face, his long black hair swishing wildly as he leaned into me, shouting every insult he could muster. Spit smacked me on my cheeks and lips as his insults escalated.

"That's it. I'm not talking to you like this," I firmly stated as my insides liquefied. Terrified, I ran down the stairs to get my purse, scared his violence would escalate and I'd be hurt—or worse. Running out of the house, him following close behind, I got to my car and frantically jiggled the door. Locked. Crying, I fished wildly in my purse for my keys. He walked to the passenger side and put his key in the lock. "You're not going anywhere without me," he said, a cruel tone masking the rage in wait.

Running back into the house, I grabbed the phone next to the couch to call for help. He tackled me onto the couch, and we struggled. He overpowered me and grabbed the phone, smashing it against the wall behind the couch. Sobbing, I got to my feet and ran to the other side of the living room, the coffee table between us.

Crying, he suddenly begged, "Please don't go. Don't leave me. You can't leave me. You know I love you."

Edging myself slowly around the table with an eye on the front door, my thoughts scrambled. "You know I'm not going to leave you. I just want to get us a little help."

"I love you," he screamed and lunged at me, knocking the table on its side. Struggling to escape his grasp, his fingers dug into my upper arms. He lifted and threw me back onto the couch. Pinning me down, his knee in my abdomen, fingers gripping my arms, his face leaned over me, rage fully exposed, eyes knitted closely together, his breath hot on my face.

I went limp and pleaded, "You're hurting me. I can't breathe. Please, please, get off me!" His hand gripped tighter. Eyeing me, he tied my wrists with the phone cord dangling on the back of the couch. He dropped his forearm across my throat, pivoting his shoulders and winding his right fist up and back over his head. Instinctively, I bit down on his forearm as hard as I could.

He gasped in surprise and grabbed his arm, rubbing it. In that same instant, I jumped up. He chased me into the dining room, shouting accusations. "You're sleeping around. I just know it!"

Trying to snap him into reality, I shouted back, "Didn't your dad do this very same thing to your mom? This very same scene? Accusing her of sleeping around?"

Jumping across the dining room table and trying to grab me, a fury exploded in his face. I slipped under his grasp and ran upstairs to the bedroom to get to a telephone, but he burst through the door just as I tried to slam it closed. Picking me up with another roar, he threw me on the bed as I continued screaming, "Don't touch me. Let me go!" He threw a punch near my face, but I squirmed out of reach just in time. Kneeing him in the groin, I finally got away.

Outside, I saw the stunning winter constellations. Shaking, I ran to our next-door neighbor's and pounded both fists on the door. "Mitch, Carol! Open up! Help me!"

No answer. The door to my house opened, and my husband stood there. "Come back home," he yelled. "Stop causing a ruckus out here!"

A light came on across the courtyard. "Is everything okay?" a woman asked with audible concern.

My husband tried to reassure her as I started screaming.

"Oh god, he's going to kill me!" I ran toward the woman as she waved me in, like a third base coach waving a runner home.

Once safe inside, the woman slammed the door shut, locking it behind her. "Tom, dial 911," she shouted, wrapping me in her arms. Breaking down in sobs, I sputtered out an unintelligible mix of thanks, gratitude, and terror. She smoothed my hair over my forehead. "It's gonna be all right, baby," she murmured. "You just sit here. I'm staying here with you. It's gonna be all right."

She unraveled the phone cable from my wrists. The long tail around my ankles slipped away just as I saw the blue and red emergency lights from the police cars reflected in the bay window behind me.

"They're out there talking to your man, honey."

"He's not my man." I shuddered.

"Okay then, well, you should talk to them, but we can wait a few minutes if you want. Do you want me to come out with you?"

"Yes. And I'm ready now. Let's get this over with."

Holding her hand tightly, I walked out. My husband was talking with two police officers on our front lawn, his eyes tracking me as I walked toward the group. I looked away and down, avoiding his stare.

"Are you Karen?" A kind police officer held out her hand to welcome me. "I'm Officer Sanders."

"Yes."

"Okay, I understand something happened tonight. Do you want to tell me what happened to you? Take your time." A second officer appeared next to her, holding a notebook.

"I'm going to take some notes. Take your time," he reiterated.

Taking a deep breath, I began relating what had happened that night. My voice grew stronger, and I found my anger. I let go of my neighbor's hand and became more animated, drawing diagrams in the air of where we were standing as the events unfolded. As I reenacted my attempts to escape my husband's violence, my body shuddered and flinched.

"I understand. Do you feel safe in your home now?"

"No. No way. Not a chance. I can't stay here tonight. I can't stay here for a long time." I shook my head until my neighbor gently touched my shoulder.

"Do you have someone you can call? Somewhere you can go tonight?" Officer Sanders asked.

"Yes." I thought of my sponsor. I was sure she'd pick me up and let me stay with her for a few days.

"I've also got some information here about shelters to give you, just in case. Now, I need to ask you this: do you want to press charges against your husband?"

I paused, trying to understand what that would mean. Officer Sanders continued, "You need to know that placing charges against an alleged perpetrator can sometimes escalate the situation. You could be at an increased risk of violence. I'll advise you to talk with an attorney should you decide to proceed with pressing charges."

My decision was clear. "I'm absolutely pressing charges," I said loudly. Standing straighter and taller, I knew I was done being intimidated, being in a marriage I zombie-walked into, and abandoning my sense of self. "Pressing every charge that can apply."

"Okay." Officer Sanders motioned to the two police officers talking with my now-subdued husband. "Do you want to get anything out of your house tonight?" she asked me.

"Yes. I should pack a bag."

"Officer Tanner will go in with you."

My neighbor rubbed my back. "You okay, honey, or do you want me to come too?"

"Oh, yes, please. If you would, that would be helpful."

As the three of us passed my husband and the officers, I heard one officer chuckle as he looked over his driver's license. "Your birthday is Valentine's Day? Seriously?" He snorted as he made a note.

We walked to the bedroom. I pulled an overnight bag from my closet and considered what I should pack: a few changes of clothes, a toothbrush, toothpaste, and cosmetics. Nothing much more seemed to matter; eventually, I knew I'd return, but not for a while.

I called and waited for my sponsor from my neighbor's house. Thirty minutes later, she came, breathless with worry and concern but calm, too, as she nearly always was. "Thank you for taking such good care of my friend," she said to my neighbor as we walked to her car.

I turned and threw my arms around this miraculous woman whose name I never learned. "Thank you," I whispered in her ear.

That night, settled into my sponsor's guest room, I dreamed of the green plantation house with the Kelly-green lawn and juniper trees surrounding it. Returning to the rocking bench, I swayed slowly on the porch and waited.

Closing my eyes, I breathed in the mossy air deep into my belly. Opening my eyes, I saw the sunrise in all its glorious colors: violet, magenta, pink, flame orange, gold. I smiled.

Waking up, I felt safe and warm in my sponsor's sunlight-filled home. Surrounded by an oasis of indoor plants, I smelled coffee and warm bread. In the main floor guest room, I stretched out my arms, back, and legs. I was sore everywhere, as if I had gone multiple rounds in a fighting match. A streak of sunlight shone across the bed. At that moment, I knew my life was changing again and knew something wonderful was awaiting me.

She knocked at the door. "You up? Would you like some breakfast?" She smiled warmly.

"Oh my gosh, yes," I answered, thrilled to be in her care. I got dressed to join her in the sunroom.

It was a small addition to the kitchen she had installed the previous year. Light-filled, with wall-to-wall glass windows and a greenhouse-style glass ceiling, the sunroom overlooked English-styled gardens to the left and a small pond toward the right. A mix of hydrangeas, roses, and Queen Anne's lace bloomed in their last season's show in pots along the far wall. A small indoor grove of Norfolk Island pine trees rooted in winter-themed pots welcomed all who entered. The right corner boasted a wandering wisteria, reaching up the trellis in its own pot, along the wall, and over the doorway to the kitchen, reaching farther still along the white ceiling beams and creating a lovely canopy. It was a gardener's dream, a woman's sanctuary, filling all my senses.

Dining was held in the center of the room. An antique green wrought-iron dining table and cushioned chairs offered a quaint sturdiness. In her writing corner, a vintage oak writing desk adorned with gorgeous carved cabriole legs and trifid feet tempted me to return to my townhouse to grab my journal. Instead, I sunk into the deep-cushioned dining chair as she entered the room carrying coffee, cream, and breakfast cakes on an obsidian tray.

"How are you feeling today?" she asked. "Did you sleep well?"

"Wow, I feel amazing," I answered. "Slept great, and I cannot thank you enough for rescuing me last night."

"Oh, Karen, I'm so sorry you went through all that. Here, have some coffee." She poured and passed me the cream. "I'm sure you haven't had time to think about things yet, but do you know what you want to do next?"

I took a sip and closed my eyes. Checking in on a quick body scan, I could feel relief, a tightness in my shoulders, which reminded me to relax them, and a tightened abdomen. "I definitely want to go through with pressing charges. I haven't changed my mind about that one bit. But also, I don't think I want to stay in that house anymore. It feels awful to me, and I don't think it will ever feel like home again. And that really pisses me off because it was my home that he moved into. He ruined it."

"Yes, his actions certainly did change the energy there. How can I help?"

I remembered that she had driven me to her home and that my car was still at my house. It was a gorgeous old Audi that my father had gifted me from his friend, whose daughter sold it when she left for college. It was on its last legs, though; since I'd gotten married, I'd fallen behind on the maintenance schedule for it, and it was intermittently failing to start.

"If you could drive me back so I could get my car, that would be great. Oh, wait—do you think he will be there?" I asked, a sharp pain stabbing me in the gut.

"No, he won't be there. He was arrested last night and taken to jail. So yes, let's go get your car after breakfast."

We finished and left the sunroom. Arriving back at my townhouse, I made a beeline for the keys, looking neither right nor left, and locked the door behind me. My sponsor waited until my car started, and I waved her goodbye for the day. Then I turned the wheel and again changed the trajectory of my life.

I had never so directly stood up to a man before.

Arriving nearly an hour before the scheduled hearing, I parked close to the courthouse entrance in Bel Air, Maryland. Originally built in the late 1850s, the two-story, red-brick classic revival-style building seemed to radiate a warm, open feeling that belied the emotional disputes and dramas played out within its wall each day. My sponsor was with me, and before we'd left my house, we triple-checked that I had everything I needed in my vintage tote bag: her notarized affidavit, the townhouse lease, the written statement I'd provided for my caseworker at the Sexual Assault/Spouse Abuse Resource Center (SARC) (one of the resources Officer Sanders had given me), and photos of my bruised wrists and ankles, revealing the marks left behind from the cable that bound me.

"Ready?" she asked.

I took a big inhale and then let it go. "Yes. Let's go in."

The building's interior was surprisingly filled with natural light. Soft white walls reflected the light from the open skylights and windows as we walked down the hall to the courtroom. Too early to enter, we found an alcove a short distance away with tall club chairs, a discreet spot.

Always aiming for comfort, I had planned to wear a nice pair of dress pants. On the advice of my SARC caseworker, though, I opted for a classic pencil skirt, a ruffled blouse I'd never wear except for this auspicious outing, and a blazer. Not at all my style, but then again, I was presenting a role: traumatized and abused young wife. Better to lean into the stereotypes and craft my appearance to support my case.

I fidgeted with the ruffles that fell like a waterfall down my chest. I picked lint off my skirt and studied my shoes. My sponsor watched me carefully.

"Are you still okay? Do you need anything?"

"I'm all right, just ready to get this over with."

Just then, my case was called. We turned and entered the courtroom.

Wearing an inmate's black-and-white striped uniform, my husband and his court-appointed attorney sat to my left. I was shocked to see a large bruise above my husband's right eye. Between getting out of my lease, finding a new place to leave, and preparing for the hearing, I had not considered what he had gone through and realized I didn't care. He was more of a stranger to me now than the day I'd met him, and his well-being was far from my mind. Laser-focused, I turned my attention to the judge, knowing I wouldn't leave until I had secured, at a minimum, a restraining order preventing that man from contacting me.

Listening intently to the evidence, the judge sat back and issued the restraining order. Sentencing for the other charges would happen at another hearing, as would the final divorce. This was no marriage; it was a karmic event. Elation and relief flooded my system, and I could barely see from the tears welling up in my eyes. I felt truly free. With my back pushed against a wall, I found within me not only a will to live but the courage to own myself in a way I'd always looked to others to provide.

A month later, nearly packed and released from the lease on the townhouse, I was ready to move into a custom log cabin as a month-to-month tenant. Still working in Baltimore, I gathered my lunch bag on a typical Monday morning and turned the key in the Audi ignition. Nothing. Not even a *wrrr-wrrr-wrrr* cranky grind indicating a drained battery. I tried a few more times without luck. My long maintenance neglect had finally caught up, and the car was done. I went back inside, called to tell work I wasn't coming in, and called my sponsor again for advice.

"I know a guy who works for a Toyota dealer. Dan—he's in the program. Here's his number. Give him a call, and I'm sure he can check out your car and help you out."

I'd met Dan once or twice and hoped he would remember me too. He did and agreed to come over after his workday to check out the car.

Dan's assessment was this: The Audi engine needed to be rebuilt. I knew I couldn't afford the labor and parts to do that. He suggested I sell the car for parts and promised to deliver a brand-new Toyota for me to try for the week. If I could come up with $1,000 as a down payment by Friday morning, I could keep the car.

I put an ad in the local paper to sell the Audi for $1,000 cash.

By Thursday evening, I had no responses to the ad. The phone didn't ring once. Disappointed, I said aloud to no one in particular, "Well, I guess this wasn't meant to be. I'm sure something else will work out." Weirdly, I felt fine—secure that something would work out. I'd figure out how to manage. I was grateful for having the experience that week of driving a lovely new car. I figured it was too late to call Dan, so I made a mental note to call him in the morning and arrange for the car's return to the dealership. At that moment—the moment I let go and felt certain that something would present itself as a solution—the phone rang.

I looked at the time: 10:05 p.m, pitch-black outside. I picked up the receiver. "Hello?"

On the line, an anxious female asked, "Hi, are you the lady selling the car?"

"Uh, yes. It's still available." (I wasn't used to being addressed as a lady.)

"Oh, thank God. I'm a mom with four kids, and my car just died. I could really use that car."

"Well, ma'am, this car doesn't run. I'm selling it for parts only. I'm so sorry."

"No, you don't understand. It's an Audi, right?"

"Yes."

"Well, my husband is an Audi mechanic. If it's not too late, we can come over right now with a flatbed tow truck and $1,000 cash."

A straight-up miracle.

I couldn't believe it. I stammered out the address and grabbed my keys to make sure all my belongings were out of the Audi. I had loved that car (especially the color: a deep eggplant purple-black) and was so grateful it would be repaired and put to good use. Shortly after I returned inside, the purchasing family arrived, all four kids in tow. While the husband-mechanic stayed outside with a high-powered flashlight, inspecting the car and the engine, I invited the young mother and her four kids in for hot chocolate.

She was so young, with thinning, straight auburn hair. You could tell she was an early bloomed beauty, but the kids and time had already eroded her youth. Thanking me for the hot cocoa, keeping a strict eye on her brood, who were delightfully entranced with the different-sized marshmallows I'd offered them, she anxiously awaited a sign from her husband.

He knocked on the back sliding glass door, and I waved him in. "Hi," I said cheerfully. "What do you think?"

"Well, ma'am, it's a solid car and nothing I can't fix. She's a beaut. You sure about selling her?"

I smiled. "Oh, absolutely. I'm really glad you can fix it and keep it running. It's more than I need, and if you think your family could put it to good use, I'm really glad for you to have it."

You could just see the relief flood the couple's faces. Beaming, eyes tearing up, the woman reached into her purse and pulled out an envelope. "One thousand dollars cash?"

I held out my hand. "Yes, that's exactly what I needed for the car. Thank you."

The oldest of her kids, maybe eight, looked up and asked, "Do we get a new car?"

"Yes, we do, Son," his father replied. "This nice lady here is helping us out."

"Oh my gosh, you are helping me more than you know!" I exclaimed.

I stood and walked the family out the front. Just before she stepped outside, the mother turned and suddenly hugged me. "Thank you," she whispered. Her husband turned too and shook my hand.

"Best of luck to you," I said. "Let me know if you have any questions!"

I shut and locked the door, stunned at how naturally and easily the transaction had fallen into place. In the morning, the new Toyota was mine—the first time I'd ever bought a car for myself—and everything had just fallen into place without me pushing, manipulating, or forcing anything to happen.

Landing

Waking up in the final week of my townhouse rental, I was excited to explore the town of Havre de Grace, where a friend lived. I planned to tour a few apartments that were coming available. Eager to leave the townhouse, which at this point felt like a B-list horror movie set, I was ready to restart this next phase of my life in this picturesque town near the top of the Chesapeake Bay.

One apartment in particular intrigued me. It was in an old ship captain's home from the turn of the century, complete with a wraparound deck, a fireplace in every room, and a large common kitchen.

Which charming Victorian home would I pick? I felt like Alice approaching a new wonderland.

Possibilities seemed endless. I imagined wearing sheer, lacy white gowns to bed with a fire lit in the bedroom fireplace and a cup of hot tea on the antique nightstand. I saw myself luxuriating after work in deep claw-footed tubs. My imagination ran wild with romantic notions based on readings of Emily Brontë and Jane Austen. Not once did I imagine the loneliness of moving again as a solitary woman to a town the locals sarcastically named "Have a Disgrace."

I was early to my first appointment, so I parked and walked to a pay phone in Concord Point Park, near the Havre de Grace Decoy Museum, and called my parents. It was a

Sunday, so I figured they would be home, and it had been about a week since I'd last checked in.

My mom answered. "Hi, Karen! What are you up to?"

"Well, I'm in Havre de Grace looking at a few apartments."

"Where? Where in the world is Havre de Grace?"

"It's a little farther north than where I've been, closer to the top of the Chesapeake, you know, on the water. It's pretty. They have a decoy museum here! I think that's a big hobby here for people."

"What do you mean, 'decoy'?"

"Oh, you know, those little wooden carvings of water birds, like ducks and such."

"No, I don't know. Karen, what in the world are you doing there?"

"What do you mean, Mom?"

"You are not a country girl. You are a city girl. What are you doing in the middle-of-nowhere Maryland?"

Her words pounded in my head like a sledgehammer.

"Karen, why don't you just come home? You can stay here for as long as you'd like. Your father and I will leave you be. Just come home, save your money, and then figure out what you want to do next."

Her tone was sharply matter-of-fact. It was not gentle or subtle; it never was. But she was right. As soon as she said it out loud, I knew at once that I didn't belong here.

"Are you sure? If so, I think yes, you're right! It would be great to come back to Virginia. Thank you, Mom."

"We'll talk soon. Start figuring out what you need to bring here and a date you'll move home, and we'll get things ready. Talk soon."

Hanging up, I let out a big sigh and turned around. Looking up at the sky, I saw bright white clouds like I'd never seen them before. I studied the park, the crystal water of the Bay, and the quaint houses in town. So pretty. So picturesque! But no, I didn't belong here. She was right. This might be a nice place to visit for a weekend, but not the place for me to live.

By this time, you know, I'd started experimenting with the "Dating How Your Grandmother Would Instruct You" and was seeing four different men: John, an IT manager who liked to go to museums, movies, and walk around DC; Stewart, a serious attorney who had box seats at The Kennedy Center Opera House; Frank, a fed and a cyclist I'd met during a few rides organized by the Potomac Pedalers cycling club; and Bill, a mechanical engineer and ethnic food enthusiast. They all had different, fascinating interests and personalities, and it was easy to meet each of them for different things, enjoy the time together, and avoid romantic entanglements.

When it came time for me to pack and move, I assumed most of them would be more than willing and able to help. I arranged a move date, secured a storage unit near my parents' town, rented a twenty-foot U-Haul truck, and called the guys for help. We had two locations from where we needed to pick up furniture and boxed items: my current townhome and a storage unit a few miles away. Similarly, when we arrived in Virginia, only a smattering of boxed items would need to be moved into my room in my parents' home, with the remainder being unloaded and efficiently stored in a new storage facility in Virginia. This would require expert planning and truck-packing, neither of which I had any talent for.

On move day, I prepared two large pots of coffee and picked up a dozen assorted donuts. Lining up enough coffee mugs, spoons, cream, and sugar, with paper plates and a roll of paper towels standing in for proper napkins. I waited with a low-grade excitement tingling just below my collarbone. Stepping into the first-floor powder room, I checked my reflection in the mirror. No makeup—after all, makeup would just make me look like I was trying too hard. I swished my hair side to side, flipped it over once and back, and ran my fingers through it, going for a slightly sexy, messy look. *Hmm*, I thought. *My lips are always dry.* Applying a thin covering of nude lip gloss to my lips, I took a final peek at myself. *Okay. Presentable without looking like I tried.*

The doorbell rang. When I reached for the doorknob, it dawned on me that I hadn't told any of these guys I was seeing the others. I swallowed a giggle, thinking, *Well, this is going to get interesting*, and opened the door.

John stood in the entranceway, a big grin on his face, a baseball cap hiding his thinning brown hair. "Good morning!" He stepped inside and gave me a hug. "Excited?"

"Yes! Hi! Thanks for coming over to help! I've got coffee and donuts over there." I pointed to the kitchen counter.

"Great! You know I love donuts." He smiled. "Great to see you."

"It is, John. Good to see you too. Listen, there's something I should tell you. I've asked a few other male friends to help me, so you'll meet everyone."

"Oh! So, I'm not your only 'male friend'?" John asked, amused.

"Oh, I mean, stop. It's not like that, you know. We're all just friends here, and there's a lot to do, so I mean, it's really great everyone could help," I stammered out a little awkwardly. *I really should have invited some women friends to help*, I thought in retrospect.

"I parked the truck in the parking lot just out the back," I said, pointing through the dining room and the large sliding back door. "And you'll see that I managed to back it in properly so it will be easier to load."

"You're a badass, you know?" John laughed.

"What? It's a big truck, sure, but I don't know. It was

easier to drive than I thought."

Another knock at the door. "Come in, it's open!" I yelled.

Bill strode in. Taller than John, he reached out his hand as I introduced the two men.

"Coffee, Bill?" I asked.

"Thanks," he said, smiling, and turned to John, making small talk. Between the two, John was the chattier one, an extrovert and a storyteller. I was impressed that Bill initiated the conversation and watched his body language as John entertained, waving his arms in an animated tale.

Frank tapped on the sliding glass door, and I waved him in. The tallest of the four men, he had a natural cyclist's build, with long legs, lanky. After introductions and coffee, he took the lead, asking the others if they'd seen the upstairs yet.

"Oh, no. I haven't taken them up yet. I thought I'd wait until everyone arrived," I said.

"Well, it's nearly nine o'clock, and from the looks of the boxes stacked up here, we've got our work cut out for us. Let's go take a look, okay?" John and Bill followed him up the stairs.

"All the boxes I could move downstairs by myself are in the living room," I called up. "It's mostly furniture and things I couldn't carry down."

Ding-dong, the doorbell rang. *Ahh, Stewart.* I smiled as I answered the door. "So glad you could come and help, Stewart! Good morning, and welcome. Would you like coffee?"

"You really live quite a drive from the District," Stewart said. "Yes, please. I can't believe you've been making this drive every time we see a concert!"

"Oh, I love driving and don't mind it one bit. A few of my other friends just went upstairs to survey the goods. Come on up, and I'll introduce you. Oh, but first, yes, coffee." I smiled.

Handing him a cup, we went up to join the others.

Introducing Stewart, I could sense a new element in the air: testosterone. Frank continued with the move strategy, but I had underestimated John's competitiveness. He probed and questioned Frank's approach. It seemed like friendly jousting. Bill roamed around the edges, peeking in the second bedroom and the baths, and eventually leaned against the main bedroom door frame, amusedly watching the two argue and banter.

Stewart tapped Bill on the elbow and pointed to a few larger wardrobe boxes. Bill nodded, and they moved the big items downstairs without a word. It was as if they'd done this a thousand times. Natural teammates, they left the posturing to the other two.

Torn between feeling I might need to referee the two upstairs and helping the two on the first floor, I bounced up and down the stairs, seeing where I could be helpful, monitoring the low-grade argument upstairs, and moving things along.

"Frank! John! Okay, how should we handle the bedroom furniture?" I asked, ready for actual progress. An hour had passed, and nothing had moved into the truck.

Bill had quietly come up behind me with a measuring tape in his hand. "I took measurements of the truck interior," he said and started measuring the big pieces of furniture.

"Wait a minute here, now, Bill. I think Frank and I have it figured out," John protested.

"Well, you know, John, I'm an engineer, and there's a right way and a wrong way to fit all these things in that space. Gimme a minute, and I'll have it laid out for you all."

John stepped back, glanced wryly over at Frank, and waited. After several more minutes of careful measurements, Bill said to the group, "Okay. Bedroom furniture goes in first; then we'll layer boxes around it all. Living room furniture goes in next, boxes laid on top and around, and we'll still have room for that small . . . you said it was small, right, Karen?" He glanced at me. I nodded. "Okay then, we have room for the rest of the stuff in that small storage locker. Let's get at it."

Leaving the guys to their plan, I went back downstairs to ensure a clear path through the back sliding door. It was a clear and warm October day, perfect for leaving the door open. Stewart was pouring a second cup of coffee, and I joined him.

"So, these are your friends?" Stewart asked, smiling, brown eyes wide under slightly raised eyebrows.

"Well, yeah, these guys are my friends," I said, smiling back.

"Oh, okay, like how we're friends? Or you know, just friends-friends?" His voice remained friendly, curious, digging for more.

"Come on now, Stewart. You know we're all friends here," I said, laughing. "And we've got a job to do, so let's go!" I deflected and dodged.

We got busy packing the truck. I loaded up boxes on trolleys, and the guys did the heavy lifting and engineering for each piece of furniture, each box. Things like plants that I didn't want in the truck were loaded into my car until it looked like a mobile jungle. By midafternoon, the townhouse was echoing, emptied of its contents. The pizzas and sodas came just before my team of suitors became hangry. Sweaty, we dove into the food, which disappeared within minutes. After a quick cleanup, we caravanned a few miles down the road to the storage unit, which held my gardening supplies, hiking and camping gear, and my bike.

"Oh, this won't take long. We'll be out of here in ten minutes," John said with confidence.

"What's in these boxes? Good god, girl, they weigh a ton.

What's in them, rocks?" Frank asked.

"Umm, actually, yes," I answered. "Rocks and bricks. I use them to line my gardens."

"Girl, we're not moving rocks." John laughed. The others nodded emphatically.

"What were you doing, paying to store rocks?" Stewart shook his head in disbelief.

"I don't know. I just really liked them! I had them in a garden I built in Virginia and really just loved it. Are you sure we can't take them?"

Bill looked at me like I'd lost my mind. "No." He laughed.

I sighed and then realized they were right. It was so weird how attached I'd become to common rocks and bricks, but then again, they were from a garden I'd built when I moved into my very own place, sober, a garden full of dreams.

I landed back in Virginia, in the home I moved into at the beginning of the end of my former life, the beginning of my maturity into alcoholism and addiction, and the arrest of my growth as a young human woman. Amazingly, I stayed sober, even in the environment where I'd found so much pain and booze. The antique liquor cabinet was in the same place in the formal living room. My parents remained the same people, sitting in the same places around the kitchen table, in their comfy seats in the living room, watching the same sorts of shows on TV. My mother kept her word, though; she and my father gave me lots of space and asked no questions. We all worked on simple common courtesy, which, in the end, was enough.

I moved a few of my favorite books, records, clothes, and cosmetics into the room I lived in at sixteen. I remembered that there was an outlet next to the bed where I could plug in a reading lamp, so I pulled the bed away from the wall and saw a black four-inch burn mark in the wallpaper, which stopped me cold. It took a minute for me to figure out that I had probably been smoking in bed and nearly set my bed on fire.

It was important for me to create a sense of community for myself, and that felt a little daunting, as my lodging was temporary. The person I'd relied on for so long, my sponsor, moved to Maui, many time zones away. But that opened up space filled with a new sisterhood in my friend Kathleen. We met through work, being assigned cubicles next to each other. We'd have lunch a few times a week together and started walking through the office complex, telling each other our stories. She had grown up in the US, South Korea, and then the foothills of Mt. Washington, New Hampshire.

Kathleen was a knitter, raised by a blue-ribbon master knitter herself. She was kind enough to teach me how to knit, and I spent many Sundays on her red couch as I struggled with the stitches. Knitting became a sort of metaphor for my life. The more I spent in the physical world, feeling the lusciousness of the high-quality fibers running between my fingers, the more my spirit healed. I made constant mistakes: tension uneven, too tight, dropping stitches, losing my place in the pattern because I was distracted. But with each mistake, Kathleen's natural reassurance opened a channel of kindness toward me in my heart, and I relaxed more and opened to the concept of simply learning instead of judging myself so harshly.

In my family, my sister had been the naturally athletic one. The story I told myself (and others) was that I had a lot of heart but not a lot of athletic skill. Having been born with that custom set of legs, they simply weren't built for and wouldn't support the typical kinds of sports a woman my age did: running, gymnastics, soccer, dance, tennis. But I found weightlifting. Lifting heavy iron with heavy-metal music, so atypical for a woman of my age, weight, and stature, brought me into my body like nothing else had. My experiences in the physical aspects of this world had never been pleasant overall, but somehow lifting weights offered healing to my body. I didn't need to look cute. I didn't need the right outfits. I didn't need to be fast. I could go to a warehouse gym, sign in wearing whatever torn T-shirt and comfortable lower bits I wanted, tie my hair back, pick up weights, and disappear not into the ether but into the feeling of my muscles working. I could feel my body. I was aware of my breath, when I held it, what the experience of it letting go felt like. I finally came into this world, feeling trust in all of myself, my senses, my right-sized judgment, everything my skin held in place. I finally landed here and was home.

The Trifecta of Ts

Not once had I closely examined what I wanted in life. Until this point, the pattern of my life revolved around jobs and men, men and jobs, moving me all over the Chesapeake Bay region. My world orbited around a trifecta of Ts—trade (jobs), testosterone (men), and treasure (money)—and I judged my self-worth based on how I fared in each of those areas.

Each offered a false sense of security, validation, and prestige. All of that rang hollow, though. Despite remaining sober and inching closer to the dreaded thirty at age twenty-eight, I reeled from the vacuous hole inside me that I secretly feared would always remain.

A few journal pages later, I ask, "Why is it that all my issues seem to surround men and my jobs? This journal is filled with each trial, just as I reach a crisis or new level of a 'breaking point.'" A few pages later, I write, "I'm reeling with anger and rage, old deep wounds; they never completely heal, do they?"

I'd forgotten that I'd fallen back into that familiar pattern! I'd find a relationship that was *doomed*, become fixated, and when it blew up, quickly find a *doomed* job until that blew up.

I began to ask myself, *What could be different? What*

would be possible if I changed this pattern?

I asked myself what I wanted in this life.

I began searching for a job that would not be the end-all challenging, fascinating job I'd always sought but instead would simply offer something ordinary, something in a healthier environment than what I'd accepted in the past. I considered how differently it would be if I'd placed the job search into the hands of God (which I was not comfortable with and could not acknowledge out loud), but I renamed the Universe, or perhaps Fate, trusting that I would be placed where I could contribute to the greater good. If that would happen, I would be willing to commit myself to one year of spiritual study, working with teachers I assumed would appear as I became ready, and continue growing my spirituality through action.

Immediately, my brain pushed back. *But what about sex?* my body cried out. *Well, what about it? I mean, I could just "get in touch" with a more intimate experience myself.* Oooof. How disappointing!

Okay then, but what about dating? my brain countered. Well, I thought that should all be limited, starting with *None*. Then when I reach a better balance, I could talk to my sponsor about how to approach the subject. I knew in my heart I was too lonely, horny, and vulnerable. Not to mention that I nearly swooned like a damsel in the 1900s every time I smelled a good cologne on a decent man. I'd have to wait until that all passed, when I felt stronger, less apt to be swept up in a rush of hormones.

Later, when the feeling of need passed and I reached a calmer place where I could access discernment and think about my own needs, yes. I contemplated dating like a grandmother would want for her youngest grandchild. No dinners. Lots of activities. Maybe a casual lunch. But absolutely no kissing or sexual contact. Time and space to get to know someone. And it might be very wise to date multiple people with different backgrounds, personalities, styles, and interests. See what I get curious about and what I'm interested in and have many experiences. Kind of like what I'd done with the guys who moved me back to Virginia, but this time, with more transparency and honesty. I hadn't been truly honest with any of those men that I was dating multiple people, and that became embarrassingly obvious when I used them for free moving labor. I wanted to be a better person this time. A woman who operated with integrity.

I realized I had never thought intentionally about these things. I had simply accepted whatever came my way, and the only way I felt valid as a person was through the work I was awarded and the men who expressed some attraction to me. Interestingly, both validation sources also colored my relationship with money and eroded my confidence in managing my personal finances. I only accepted what a job offered me and tried to "make do" with what that was. It never occurred to me to figure out what a market rate was for my skills and to ask for what I wanted. Like I did with men, I simply tried to adjust myself to someone or something else's reality, never exercising choice. I didn't know I had a choice.

Having space from men gave me room to examine other parts of my life. I had been in a cycle of debt ever since I left my parent's home, and I couldn't figure out why that was. I felt so ashamed about that. The story I'd adopted from my family was that I would never be able to manage money, that I was clearly incompetent in some insurmountable ways when it came to personal financial matters. There was also an unwillingness to live within my means. My father often quoted one of his friends, who believed anyone struggling with managing their finances simply refused to grow up and deal with reality. When it came to money and my own abilities to act like an adult in that area of my life, I simply believed I was at fault, was deficient, and felt baffled and deeply ashamed. So yes, that was another part of my life that I disowned out of feeling overwhelmed and uncertain, and I longed for a partner who would be much more skilled and take that part over for the betterment of us both.

I called my sponsor, full of despair and frustration at my lack of progress. "You know, I've now been clean and sober for over seven years, and I seriously don't know what's wrong with me that I can't get this right! Why haven't I made better progress with my money?"

"Oh, sweetie." Her voice was like a hug coming over the line. "Do you remember the money sessions we had at my house nearly every single Sunday when you were new in sobriety?"

Oh, wow. I'd forgotten about those early days in my first year of sobriety.

"I was completely overwhelmed, too, trying to figure out how to make ends meet! That was just after Adam—you remember that a-hole of a husband of mine—you know, he had been a chemical engineer with Dow Chemical. We never had money problems."

"I'd forgotten about that!"

"Oh, yeah. He easily took care of us, even after we had those three rugrats!"

"Right. I remember your kids were so young."

"Uh-huh. I had three right in a row, and you were there holding me when Crystal was born! But yeah, remember when he abruptly left not only his job but the entire industry to become a drug and alcohol counselor? Honorable to some, maybe, but it financially devastated us when his income dropped nearly ninety percent."

"Oh my gosh, I didn't realize he took such a salary hit."

"Well, yeah, sweetie. I mean, it's great to help people, but not at the expense of your own responsibilities. I was so angry with him. He didn't even give me a heads-up that he was thinking about making such a drastic change. And remember, I didn't have any job training or practical, employable skills. I'd only been a fashion model in Beverly Hills in my twenties and a sculptor in the past. We suddenly went from no money concerns to being on welfare, like, overnight."

"So every Sunday, you would come to my house, and we would hand each other our budgets. I didn't have any emotional or shame-based ties to your budget, Karen, and I could easily see options and solutions you couldn't. Remember? I told you that you didn't need to buy coffee at the grocery store but could drink free coffee at meetings. And I taught you to use a sponge and a cup instead of Tampax! Every little bit helped, and you made so much progress in a year! I was so proud of you. And you could see solutions to my budget too. I was so freaked out about it, especially since I had three little kids."

"Right! It really helped me feel useful, helping you. Sharing our budgets with each other also tore down those iron castle gates of shame that had held me hostage for so long."

"Oh, me too! And you know it doesn't matter how long you've been sober. I always need help with things like that."

I paused, thinking about how much that experience taught me the value of asking for help, being willing to be seen in a vulnerable state, and the incredible relief I found in not having to have everything figured out.

Suddenly filled with gratitude, I told her, "You know, just meeting with you every week helped me drop this sort of icy mask I was trying to keep up. It wasn't real; I didn't have my shit together and felt completely lost. But for my entire life, I felt like I had to look like I knew what I was doing, which is a form of deceit. It also gave me a first glimpse into how safe you made me feel by being real. You helped me gain confidence and open myself to asking for help, which was a bold new idea for me."

"Aww, I know, sweetie! Same for me, and you know, even though I have been sober a few more years than you, I'd never been faced with the type of economic ruin Adam put us through. So you helped me just as much. I love you!"

We hung up, and I thought about how significant that time had been for me. Before I quit drinking and drugging, asking for help was a death sentence. It showed I was weak and a failure. Seeing how that worked now in my life, I began to benefit from the strength it brought me, and it opened the door to many new people with whom I could share and receive.

Years later, as I sat down on a Sunday, with all those lessons banked in my experience and confidence in my capability, I engaged in what I called a rather "sobering" session at the computer working on my finances. Much improved from the usual terrifying session I previously experienced! I realized that the panic and shame I had felt my entire life was gone. A fleeting feeling of fear, and then it passed. I suddenly knew that, in time, I would turn a corner and feel competent and successful in this area of my life. Yay me! Another part of me is seen, known, owned, and celebrated.

After a second marriage crashed and burned, I found myself financially devastated. I had turned my financial well-being to a man I desperately wanted to believe would take care of me. With my two young boys looking to me for survival, I surrendered to the fact that it would be me who would save myself. I created a spreadsheet that tracked every single bit of income coming my way and when it would arrive, budgeting every dollar based on priority needs. After carving our expenditures as drastically as possible in the

Washington, DC, metro area, Kathleen suggested I meet with a financial adviser at a local banking and investment firm for advice. Great idea. I called and made an appointment.

Bringing hard copy printouts of my financial statement, computer in tow, I sat in the office waiting room until the adviser called me in.

"Great to meet you. I'm grateful for your help."

"No problem. It's good to meet you too. So, what brings you in today?"

After giving her enough context about my background and self-held beliefs, I shared how hard I had worked to gain expertise in managing my finances. I gave her a copy of my financial statement and opened my computer so she could see how I was managing my cash flow.

"Wow. This is impressive, Karen. Actually, it's far more exact and detailed than I have my clients track. You're doing everything I would advise a client! Where did you learn all this?"

"Well, mostly from experience and research. This is what seems to work for me and the family so far. But honestly, I feel like I'm missing something. I can't seem to get ahead and build a safety net, so we're always so close to the edge. I can't figure out what I'm doing wrong."

"You're not doing anything wrong, Karen. What you need to do is make more money."

Oh! Blessed revelation! I could do that. It was a relief to hear the confirmation that I was doing things right. And what a simple solution: make more money! Plus, because of all the work and analysis I had done, I could easily decipher how much more money I needed to create stability. I was filled with a renewed energy and a cautious hope.

I have a complicated relationship with hope. Hope can feed denial. It can keep me from being present when I get hooked on dreams. I get it mixed up with magical thinking, losing myself in a half-dream state so natural to live in. It reminds me of reading in that white wicker rocker high up in the tree line of our deck. The present moment is a toss away, an afterthought of what I dream will come. It's a place I never reach but always long for.

Doing the footwork and being willing to work, research, and take action has become my grounding force for hope.

Part 3

spir·it / [Willingness]

"A woman in harmony with her spirit is like a river flowing. She goes where she will without pretense and arrives at her destination prepared to be herself and only herself."

—Maya Angelou

Velveteen

After all this work, this journey, the therapy, the sobriety, I wondered what it would be like to just love all the parts of *me*. What would be possible if I gave myself love, acceptance, gentleness, and tenderness and cherished each part of myself? Even the things I never liked, starting with my name that briefly became a meme encompassing all the ugliness of privilege and entitlement of the White American woman? What if I welcomed all the parts of myself that I never wanted to acknowledge—the insecurities I have about my body, my appearance, my teeth so permanently stained by Tetracycline, and the parts that created deep psychological damage and self-loathing about my smile—for the rest of my life?

The belly that I dreamed of slicing off so I could have as flat an abdomen as everyone else and say, they had that perfection, so flat and straight, hip bones protruding up as the standard. No, no, I never had that. Mine was always soft like a gentle pillow. The perspective of my younger self, always demanding that I become different from I was, more like the other girls, rejecting the whole of me, my body, my skin, my anxiety, my emotions that I felt so violently through my limbs and torso, like wild stampeding Mustangs running freely through the plains—what if . . . what if I just accepted it all?

The inner parts of me . . . the parts I tried to hide, my innermost secrets, the Tasmanian devil part of me, whipping me into frenetic action to calm rising anxiety. The relentless judgmental part of myself, who I named "Judy McJudge-Judge," continuously judged me, others, and any situation, drawing conclusions that nearly always left me feeling alone, served as an overstepping mechanism, trying to always keep me safe.

Life isn't safe. Life is real. What would it be like to be real?

The Bad Girls Club

I first found girls and women like me in the meeting rooms of Twelve Step programs. We were born from many circumstances: illegitimate, affairs, one-night stands; born to teenagers; born to generational wealth; born from war zone traumas; and born with hope and without it. We came from everywhere with every possible story you can imagine. But we ended up in exactly the same place: loathing ourselves, tearing ourselves apart with lifetimes of shame, unable to help ourselves, hopeless, and lost in a forever state of downward spiral. You could easily see it in some of us, like me: grossly underweight, dead eyes, jaundiced pallor, and an indifference to personal hygiene. For others, her inner dying was hidden behind stately, accomplished careers and homes, everything just peachy until you looked closely at her eyes.

We were young adults and older women working in corporate C-suite roles, prostitutes, servers, recruiters, poets, bartenders, nannies, musicians, homemakers, members of the military, members of the government, attorneys, and wanderers. We arrived in the rooms after years of trying and failing, trying and not fixing whatever was wrong with us on the inside. Some of us already knew we were addicted to things that hurt us, but we couldn't stop the addiction to it, be it alcohol, drugs, spending, food, gambling, destructive sex, or love—name your poison. I learned that I was addicted to alcohol and drugs after that intervening October day. That news came with complete relief and clicked into place inside of me like a missing puzzle piece, answering all the terrible circling questions about what was wrong with me. I was so bone-tired from trying to live like a normal person, and that's impossible when you've fallen apart so completely, physically, emotionally, mentally, and spiritually. How luxurious it felt to completely surrender and not try to be anything I wasn't anymore.

In 1985, the year I was able to find grace in recovery and become free from alcohol and drug consumption, the participation in and adherence to the framework that the Twelve Step program offered to me was the only commonly accessible path to sobriety. In the United States, it was squarely at the height of the "war on drugs" Reagan years when First Lady Nancy Reagan headlined the Just Say No anti-drug campaign. It was a laughable and terrifying time, moralizing drug use and severely punishing drug users, especially people of color, with no acknowledgment, research, or services addressing the disease model of alcoholism and addiction. And the more time I put together as a clean and sober woman, the more stunningly unique I found the circumstances by which I was given the grace to quit. It occurred to me that that was probably a one-time deal, and I may never have another opportunity to quit again should I decide to pick up a drink or drug. Over the years of attending meetings and watching some people suffer from chronic relapse patterns, it dawned on me that I may not be so lucky as to die from this disease; rather, I might just stay out there, getting sicker and sicker and sicker, older, skankier. I imagined myself as a hopeless street woman, too old and sick to work, a barfly sitting at the end of a small dive bar in the dirty basement of some tenement building in the outskirts of DC, with long, stringy gray hair, missing teeth, abscesses in my skin, and ragged clothes hanging off me, completely delusional, hitting on some twenty-five-year-old man, gravelly whispering from rotting teeth, "Hey, baby, buy me a beer," thinking I was hot like some twenty-something from decades past. I'm certain that would be my future—or some version like that.

The education I obtained about the disease model from the treatment center was worth any admission price. As an addict suffering from a compulsion to use, an obsession to drink, and an allergy of the body, without healing, there was nothing I would experience other than the continuation of the obsession-compulsion cycle. More frightening was how the disease progressed, which I could see during my work in treatment with Charles and studying my history. The generational impact of addiction and alcoholism was clear as I learned more about my family. Sobering up gave me new eyes through which I could see my immediate family and the grip addiction held on them.

After returning to the Washington, DC, area from treatment in Charlotte, I gravitated to Twelve Step program meetings that had younger people, people like me. I just could not identify with the older men and women who made up the more established meetings. I was obsessed with my youth and wanted so desperately to know that I would still have a future, still have fun, and find love that would last me a lifetime, and hanging around younger people seemed to fill that need. But over my first year, I saw that the meetings I attended just didn't have the strength, deep wisdom, and longevity of the more established community, and I slowly began attending more of those meetings and found, despite outward appearances, age differences, or lifestyles, my people there.

This is not at all to say that I think the Twelve Step

model is the only way to stop drinking and stay clean. Since the American Medical Association classified alcoholism as a disease in 1953, and included addiction in that medical classification in 1987, research in this area exploded, resulting in dozens and dozens of recovery models, including:

- Medical detox
- Rehabilitation: online, inpatient, and outpatient
- Holistic recovery
- Cognitive behavioral therapy (CBT)
- Contingency management for addiction
- Recovery Dharma
- Rational emotive behavior therapy
- Motivational interviewing
- Couple and/or family therapy
- Twelve Step facilitation
- EMDR
- Dialectical behavior therapy, including harm reduction
- Matrix model for addiction
- Person-centered therapy
- Recovery and trauma-informed coaching
- Plant-based medicine therapies such as ayahuasca ceremony

...And so many more.

Years and years after my recovery began, I met Maria, Angie, and several of the other middle school girls I used to smoke with outside that schoolyard gate. We reunited over lunch and realized we were the surviving members.

Laughingly, we called ourselves *The Bad Girls Club* and decided we needed to stay in touch. Angie and Maria ordered wine and shared their stories. They each had created a drug-free life that worked for them. They thrive in their careers, enjoy relationships, travel, and feel a satisfaction that suits them. However, like so many women with addiction in their past, they sometimes still struggle with resentment, shame, guilt, and doubt at a deep level.

Angie's life had changed dramatically. Growing up without a father, she talked about how she craved the love of a man and became a moderately promiscuous teenager. Yet in all her relationships, she kept one foot out the door. Married shortly after she started working as a dispatcher, she had two kids by the time I entered treatment. Being a good mom was important to her, and she was. However, the stress of working and being a young full-time mother took a toll on her volatile marriage, which finally ended in a blaze of whiskey, cocaine, and infidelity on both sides, screaming accusations and furious tears. A few years later, she met a bouncer, Darryl, at a club. Although she was sinking further into problematic drinking, it wasn't long before they felt they were a match made in heaven. She and her kids moved in, and she had another. Darryl was a traditional husband and expected her to keep the house clean and make dinner. In return, he provided financial support, leaving Angie's income for her pleasure. She thrived from his stable routine and structure. Over time, though, as the kids grew up, she got bored with the marriage and their arrangement.

In 2009, she met a charming and good-looking man and left Darryl before understanding that this new lover was addicted to crack cocaine. The guilt overwhelmed her, and she told herself, *Well, I've ruined my whole life, so I might as well . . . shoot, if I can't beat 'em, I may as well join 'em.*

Within the first thirty days of meeting that guy, she set herself up in a new apartment where she could smoke crack nearly around the clock. She spent $5,000 in one month, blowing through her savings and tax refund.

One day, Angie's new beau called her from the moving company where he worked and told her he'd gotten hurt on the job. "You gotta come get me, babe, to the hospital right now for X-rays."

Dropping her crack pipe, Angie grabbed her keys and drove thirty minutes to his location. She was so sick from smoking crack that she could barely breathe; she'd smoked so much crack that her lungs were burned.

"I'd gotten up that morning, dropped him at work, and went to the urgent care where they wanted to admit me for those burns on my lungs, but I knew I needed to hit the pipe again," she remembered. Arriving at Port Royal to pick up her man, she pulled into a mostly empty parking lot. No one was in sight. Angie got out, kicked a few dried cigarette butts out of her way, and scanned the warehouse parking lot. A few rusted cars were parked near a garage door. Weeds forced their way up through cracks in the asphalt. She texted the guy and waited impatiently for him to respond. *Where are you?* Her chest hurt: sharp, stabbing pains whenever she took a tight, short breath. All she wanted to do was crawl into her bed and smoke enough to feel better.

Where are you? Where are you? Where are you? she texted and paced, paced and texted. "This is ridiculous," she croaked out. She realized she had been pacing in circles and was nearly at the edge of the warehouse. Turning, she stormed back to her car, floored it to the exit, and sped home, careening recklessly in and out of two lanes of traffic, slamming on the brakes at red lights, and entering the highway twenty miles per hour over the speed limit. "Get the fuck out of my way!"

she screamed at the traffic and broke down in sobs at the searing pain ripping apart her throat.

Slamming the car into park in front of her garden apartment building, Angie sprinted up two flights of stairs to the slightly ajar door. She paused, puzzled, leaned back to double-check the unit number (212A), and then pushed open the door.

Everything was gone.

Not that she had a lot. But the furniture, her Mr. Coffee coffeemaker, the can opener her mother had given her when she first left home, the one dish towel, the coffee mug her daughter gave her on Mother's Day, the bath towels, her jewelry, her bed, and her crack pipe. All gone.

She wandered back and forth between the kitchen, the desolate, dusty living room, and the empty bedroom, staring at where her bed should have been. And that's when it hit her—that guy and his wife set her up, called her to get her to leave the apartment, loaded up one of the moving vans with all her possessions, and wiped her out.

Angie's legs buckled where her bed had been, and she collapsed on the floor. She lay on that floor for days, wanting to die, praying to get a blood clot and die. A few days later, two of her work friends arrived. Angie hadn't moved from where she'd fallen. Her oldest work friend took one look at her and said, "Girl, get your ass up off that floor and take a damn shower. We're taking you to dinner and going shopping."

You know, that had been their thing.

"Your ass is getting up off this floor, you're getting in that shower, and you're coming out with us," the other woman echoed.

So Angie picked herself up, dusted herself off, and found the determination she needed to survive. She used that determination to pivot.

Angie's not ashamed of her story at all. "You know, I walk around with a smile every day." Secretly, though, she confessed, she still struggles inside. She has always wanted to use her experiences to help others. She struggles with the trauma of the abortion she had when she was fifteen. She never forgave her ex-husband because she felt he bullied her into having that abortion.

"He told me that if I didn't abort that child, I would never see him again."

Angie still cries as she thinks about and shares this memory that has haunted her throughout her life. She recognizes that she could receive help from counseling and is on a waiting list to join a freedom group at her church. She still grieves that loss every single day, even getting a tattoo to represent that child, thinking it would help, but in the end, it didn't.

Angie's life continued for several years with a theme of loss. "You know, my husband left me for one of my friends in April 1991. But we reconciled enough for him to return home to me a few months later, in July. So, naturally, I wanted to spend as much time as I could with him, and I showered him with all my attention. Before we reconciled, though, I spent time with my mother. I was very close to my mom."

"One night in August, my mom called and asked me if I wanted to take the kids and go back-to-school shopping. But that night, you know, my husband wanted to tend our daughter's horse. Now, ordinarily, I would have gone with my mother to shop for the kids, but because I was showering that man with attention, I chose to go with him instead. My mother dropped the kids off, and we put them to bed a little before ten that night."

The phone woke Angie around four in the morning, and she learned that her mother died of an aneurysm. "The grief and the *guilt* I felt from not spending that time shopping with her was overwhelming. I'd chosen a man over my mom, and it was too late to change anything. I'd missed the last time I'd ever have with her. So now, no matter how tired I am or how much I just need to sit alone and chill after a stressful day at work, if one of my kids or grandkids calls and wants to do something, I can't say no . . . EVER." She's gripped with a fear that it could be her last opportunity to see her family alive.

Angie continues to struggle to live with what she feels is PTSD.

More than anything, Angie feels that if she can ever heal from the grief and resentment she carries, she will start a group to help other women heal. Ultimately, she's not against abortion; in her mind, it must be a choice, but it's an extremely important decision that should be a woman's decision, and hers alone, without the influence of a man. She feels like she chose a man over her child and hates herself for that.

Before Maria started working for the government, the year before her husband died, she'd always tried to be the best mom. Looking back, she realized that maybe she'd always had tendencies to reach for alcohol or drugs, but she had not been drinking or doing much of anything as a young adult; she had focused on being the best working mom she could be.

One day, she arrived at her youngest son's Little League baseball game with a horrible headache. One of the teammates' mothers saw her clenching her jaw tight and offered to help.

"I have something that could help you with that," she said, and she gave Maria a Percocet, for which she was grateful.

She quickly swallowed the pill with a sip of Gatorade, and before she knew it, the headache was gone. Sweet relief. Maria thought nothing of it; after all, she had been on different medications before with no complications.

"But you know, later in that week, I got it in my mind that the team mom had this medication, and I could get more of it from her. She would probably sell it to me; I wouldn't expect her to just keep giving it to me." *Why not?* she thought. *I mean, there's no harm in it. I mean, what is so wrong with feeling relaxed?* She didn't think it was rationalization; it seemed completely natural and made sense.

"So, looking back, I'm pretty sure that's what started my addiction to OxyContin. Eventually, I realized that I would lose my job because I got to a point where I wasn't hiding it anymore."

For a long time, she hid her dependence on the pills. But one day, her boss looked at her and said, "Maria, I have a problem with sleep. I think you might have some issues too. If you need some time, I will allow you to take a leave of absence. No one has to know."

"My husband came at once to take me home. While he was a hard-ass, he was very supportive of me, and he took care of the kids while I went to treatment in a short-term, outpatient drug rehabilitation center. You would think that was the right place to make a change, and a change did happen, yes. But not the one you were expecting."

It was in rehab where Maria met Michael, and Michael introduced Maria to heroin. "One day, we were leaving that outpatient clinic, and Michael needed to score, but he didn't have a driver's license, so he couldn't drive himself to get the dope. You know, I do love being kind and accommodating, so I offered to drive him. I had tried heroin once before, many years prior, and always held it in my mind that that was a one-time thing. I'd never thought much about it after that. But that day driving Michael, well, it all came flooding back to me—that feeling, the place that only heroin can take you, and I succumbed."

Before she knew it, she was going into withdrawal, which she was terrified of.

"And what they don't tell you, of course, when you take that first pill, and you think there's no harm in it, is how horrible the withdrawal is. I knew I was going to be sick, and I was in that place where I didn't want to use but couldn't stop, or else I'd get violently sick from withdrawals."

After some months of increasing heroin use, Maria finally opted to drive herself to the county hospital and commit herself to the psychiatric ward so she could kick her addiction. She reported that it was the worst place she had been to yet. It was loud, with periodic shrieks and mumblings from the patients full of menace and fear.

"I was afraid to go to sleep. I shared a room with a woman who peed in her bed, an awful, horrible, foul stench of urine. Each night, there was another woman who walked around the floor, wandering in and out of patients' rooms and saying all kinds of delusional things. I was left wondering every night, *Is she going to come in here and stab me?*"

Weeks passed, and Maria became more desperate for sleep, relief, and progress. Eventually, she found a really nice nurse who told her, "You don't belong here, honey. I want you to go to this addiction clinic in Silver Spring."

Maria laughed at her and said, "Are you kidding me? You want me to drive over two hours every day for outpatient treatment?"

The nurse replied, "I'm not asking you to stay there. I'm just asking you to go one time."

Meeting later that day with her doctor, he explained,

"Hey, you need to go where people are trained and skilled with addiction and recovery, and there are top specialists at this clinic."

Maria went the next day and continued for over two years. At first, she went two or three times a week, and over time, she tapered to once a week to continue care. Eventually, she became a Board member supporting the foundation the clinic built, which helped raise money to support those who were in continuing care in the community.

"There were days when I was so sick, so frustrated, and so sad, and there were obviously reasons behind that, but there were reasons, you know, for self-medicating. I had been in a very abusive marriage, and I wasn't happy with myself. I never wanted my children to think I would speak badly about their father because, in some ways, he was an amazing person. But that made it all the more difficult to trust. I was trying to bury it all, the exhaustion. I was almost like a single mother in some ways, with the responsibility of the house and the bills. But it was mostly that mental place of unhappiness and not being with the right partner. And I knew, of course, I was just trying to self-medicate. I was trying to make myself feel better but didn't know how."

Several months later, at the second lunch of our sassy club, I found myself sitting in a booth next to Mary. I wanted to make amends with her so much that I had reached out a few times over the years but hadn't succeeded. While she was cordial and polite, I think we both felt stiff as we made awkward small talk.

After drinks arrived, Mary and I raised our (nonalcoholic) iced teas with the other women in a fun toast. Turning to her,

I took a deep breath, summoned courage, and began.

"Mary, I'm so glad to be sitting next to you. I have something I'd like to tell you."

"Oh, Karen, it's so good to see you, and I'm glad we have a chance to talk!" Mary responded with an upbeat attitude.

"Thank you. You know, when we were young girls, I harmed you. I said things that were completely untrue and started terrible rumors about you. None of it was true, and..."

Mary put her hand on my arm, her eyes welling with tears. "You don't have to say anything, Karen. That was so long ago."

"Oh, I know it was years and years ago, and even though we were children, I hurt you in a terrible way. You know, your mom was right—I was sick. But that doesn't erase the fact that I made up terrible things to hurt you. For that, I am so sorry, so sorry for the pain I caused you."

"Oh, honey," Mary exclaimed softly. She leaned over, and we hugged, long-forgotten tears filling both of our eyes. It felt divinely arranged that we were seated next to each other when we were both open to healing old wounds. It was the last lingering amend on my list of people I had harmed and for whom I owed so much. Step nine of the Twelve Steps invited me to make direct amends whenever possible (except when doing so would cause further harm). Amends isn't a simple apology; I'd lived my life for so many years feeling sorry, tossing out "sorry!" like leaves blowing in the wind to avoid further calls for accountability. What freedom, though, can be realized through an honest effort to change the nature of the experience and the nature of the relationship. To offer healing through honest admission of the harm I had caused. Mary's tears revealed the hurt I had caused her that stayed with her for all these years, and my ownership of my actions—in that very moment—changed everything between us. I saw her, and she knew that I saw her and the pain that remained in her heart. All the protective walls between us came down at that moment, and we were filled with ease, lightness, and grace.

My experiences in recovery models have spanned detox and inpatient treatment, CBT, Jungian therapy, and EMDR. Because my experience of being in my body has included various forms of trauma, I've also explored multiple other modalities, including massage, Shiatsu, Reiki, acupuncture, sound and forest bathing, reflexology, Buddhist meditation, polarity treatment, heavy weightlifting, swimming in sacred waters, and simply walking in nature. All those tools and modalities helped me rewrite the story of my experience in a healthier way. More importantly, embracing my physical body and deepening my awareness, ownership, and agency of it became a crucial integration point for my mind, body, and spirit. Although my inner "toolbox" for dealing with myself and my issues began with the twelve steps, I'm grateful that the field of recovery expands now beyond the twelve steps to be more inclusive, provide more variety to address the whole person, and make recovery more accessible to the thousands of people who just don't relate to the Twelve Step model.

"If I had to pick my biggest struggle that remains today, it would be guilt," Maria remarked over another Bad Girls Club lunch with me and Angie. "One might believe that after years of making amends and therapy, I could overcome this, and in part, I have. Being forgiven by others is powerful, and in large part, I have forgiven myself too, in that I have accepted that I can't change things, even things I still feel guilty about. It's those very things that make me who I am today."

"You have nothing to feel guilty about," Angie championed. "Like me, you're a badass."

"Oh, but specifically, I feel my compassion and empathy toward others (while I always had that to some extent) were enforced by my own experiences. I know better than to judge others' actions in large part because I understand that some things can't be explained rationally with intellect. That mountain of guilt I used to try to bury was easier to navigate once acceptance and forgiveness were introduced, but it didn't disappear. It's still there, just no longer the obstacle it once was. I may have confronted the mountain and made it to the other side, but every once in a while, when I look in the rearview, I still see it standing there. It's no longer the obstacle it once was, but it still hurts to look at it. Like Joan Didion said, 'The way you got sideswiped was by going back.' And occasionally, I go back. And for me, it all circles back to my own choices and the impact they had on my sons, which were, ironically, choices made when trying to avoid the mountain of guilt and pain to begin with. I don't know if that makes sense to anyone but me?" She took a sip of her wine and glanced at us both, that question lingering.

"It makes total sense to me, Maria," I offered. "Thank you. That's so beautifully expressed. I don't think, for me at least, that the goal is to get rid of those parts of me that are obstacles; rather, like you said, it's to welcome them, see them clearly for what they are, and accept and forgive myself for all of it. And then invite those parts back inside me and bring them home."

I do not judge what recovery models work best or are most effective for each individual. I think it depends on what you want. However, in 2020, a Stanford researcher and two collaborators conducted an extensive review of Alcoholics Anonymous studies and concluded that "Alcoholics

Anonymous [is] the most effective path to alcohol abstinence" (Erickson, 2020). I'll also throw in that the spiritual opening offered by Twelve Step programs has been the most effective path for me to maintain a full recovery from addiction. Why is that?

Through my years in these programs, I've witnessed events, large and small, that offered recovery beyond simple abstinence. The time spent studying the program steps in the community opened my heart to love and healed my spirit, deepening my sense of freedom and peace and removing a lifetime of anxiety, shame, and fear. The work I've done using the Twelve Step framework made living clean and sober not only tolerable but joyfully content. I much, much prefer to live clear of mood- or mind-altering drugs. Experiencing life otherwise feels akin to walking around with dirty glasses: slightly irritating at best and obstructive to all that life has to offer at worst.

The first woman I sponsored in the program was a young woman named Cindy. I'd been sober for about eighteen months, and she was the first person who asked me to help her. Women in the program warned me about her. She was a "lost cause," a chronic relapser, too needy. She had a reputation for getting clean and then falling in love. When the relationship ended, she predictably fell apart and relapsed, and this pattern repeated over and over, year after year. Like me, she first entered the program in her young twenties. She was still quite pretty and earnest; she wanted me to help her, so I consented.

"How long have you been coming to meetings?" I tentatively asked her at our first coffee meeting. I was hesitant, worried about evoking shame or inserting unintentional judgment.

"Well, about ten years now," she responded, glancing

briefly out the window of the diner we were sitting in. "I'm thirty-one now, and I started hitting a bottom at twenty-one, so there's that. A lot of failure. But you know, I keep trying! I know I want to get this, you know. I just keep falling for the same type of guy over and over. I have a bad picker." A small shadow of a smile moved across her face. "I'm just a country girl, you know, and my mama didn't teach me any different. You go to get yourself married as soon as you finish high school, right? And you have some kids and make your home happy. That's not so bad?" Her voice ended in a question as I watched and listened. "But you know, so far, no man, no happy home, that's for sure! And no kids . . ." She trailed off, looking away.

"That's okay, Cindy, don't worry!" I reached out, gave her hand a light squeeze, and then brought my hand back to my lap. "All you have to do is not pick anything up that's mood- or mind-altering, other than, say, any health medications prescribed by your doctor, one day at a time. All you need to focus on is today. Go to a meeting today. Try to help someone today. Oh, and it doesn't hurt to pray to anything, whatever may be out there, to help you stay clean and sober today. That's it. If you do those things, I swear to you, everything will fall into place just as it's supposed to."

We went to meetings together each night for a few weeks, and I saw her beauty blossom, her eyes light up, her smiles widen a little more, and her weariness lift. I became excited each time I got in my car to pick her up, knowing I'd see her spirit shine through a little more. She and I both stayed clean in this way for several months.

On a warm, breezy May morning, Cindy called me. "Hi!" Her voice was light, nervous, and happy. "Is it okay with you if I get a ride to tonight's meeting from Jonathan?"

My brain quickly scanned for any Jonathans I'd seen in

meetings and hit on the image of one. Tall, lanky, longish dark hair, a sweet smile. I'd heard he was new in the area and had just over a year sober. Cindy was coming up on a mere five months, not enough to build a foundation that would help her avoid risking her earlier pattern of romance, rejection, and relapse.

"Who is Jonathan to you?" I asked her directly, couched in as gentle a tone as I could summon.

"Well, you know who he is, right? I mean, he's cute! And he's so nice and easy to talk to. We started talking a few times on the phone, and he just seems so nice. Is it okay for me to get to know him as a friend?"

Slippery slope, I thought. I remembered what women had warned me about early on. But then I considered my role in her life, and in my mind, it was about helping her apply the principles of faith, service, honesty, open-mindedness, and willingness to her daily life. *You can't do that if you avoid life, can you?* an inner voice questioned me.

"Well, Cindy, I don't think there's anything wrong with getting to know him as a friend. Just keep praying to anything that's out there to keep you safe. Keep up your meetings. Keep being honest with me and other women. And I think you'll be fine, as long as you stay clean and sober."

Three months later, a clean and sober Cindy and Jonathan married. Many people, both men and women, lost their minds in gossip and harsh judgment. "See?" women exclaimed. "Karen, it's just a matter of time before she relapses, and she'll probably take him down too."

"I don't know," I'd respond when I felt the gossip was getting too far out of hand. "I mean, she is still clean and sober, going to meetings, and staying in touch with me, and she seems really happy." My response was always met with sarcasm and skepticism.

A few months later, Cindy called me, excitement bursting from her voice. "Can I come over? Can we come over? We have something so great to tell you!"

She threw her arms around me, Jonathan standing behind her in the doorway, grinning the widest I'd ever seen. Eyes sparkling, Cindy cried out, "We're going to have a baby!"

"What? When?" I asked, thrilled for her.

"Well, we just found out, so it looks like I'll be a mom next April! I can't believe it!"

"Oh my gosh, congratulations to you both," I said as I swept them into a group hug. "Now, you're going to have to pay extra good attention to your health, right?" I advised as if I were her mom.

"We have a great women's doctor, ma'am," Jonathan reassured me. "And I'm taking great care of her."

"Oh, I don't doubt that for a minute, Jonathan." I smiled back at him.

Cindy's recovery and pregnancy continued smoothly until her seventh month when she was diagnosed with triple-negative breast cancer, a highly aggressive form. She stayed solidly grounded in the Twelve Steps as her new young family began, giving birth to a beautiful girl and finding true happiness in service to her family and child. She died six months later, having lived a lifetime of love and fulfillment in the last few years of her short life, removing from me any doubt that people have their paths. Who am I to judge what people should and should not do?

In the brief two years of her sobriety, Cindy found deep friendship, trust, honesty, a sense of something greater than herself with which she could depend, a loving husband who truly cared for who she was, and the ability to create, be present for, and experience that happy home and family she longed for. She lived an entire lifetime in her two years of sobriety that left me humbled and breathless with the beauty, cosmic wisdom, and faith that there's a greater individual path for each of us that we cannot see in its entirety. We can only see the next step or two and the sense of direction, perhaps from a bit of hindsight.

There are tenets in the Twelve Steps program that can be found in almost any spiritual guidebook you point at. It's helpful to keep a mind that is open, flexible, and able to learn. It's helpful to truly hear what messages are coming in. Honesty, though hard and at times scary to open to, is critical to growth and evolution. Nothing happens without willingness. I cannot think my way into healthy living; no, I must act. Isolation is a box where mold, misery, and madness grow. The most humbling experience I continue to be invited to is admitting my mistaken thoughts and actions to someone else. I'm not a fan of totally dropping my ego and self-will (I don't think humans can permanently do that); rather, I'm a proponent of aligning those with a greater spiritual purpose. After all, I am a human, incapable of removing my human parts.

There are so many things that I think make Twelve Step fellowships so incredibly special. I recognize that it's not for everyone, and I think that if you are searching for healing, for relief from alcoholism, from addiction, you will find what works for you. But I'm so incredibly grateful that the Twelve Step program was the only game in town for me when I needed it. There was so much that made me uncomfortable in the beginning, so much that I didn't relate to, that I straight-up hated, that I found cringeworthy. The hand-holding and prayer at the end of each meeting gave me the heebie-jeebies; it felt cult-like. There was the subtle and not-so-subtle message of "if you stop coming to meetings, you'll drink or use again," which in my case turned out not to be true, but I only tested that theory after attaining stable and consistent sobriety. I've seen that to be true for others, though, but I suspect there was more going on with those people than a simple absence from meetings. I didn't want to call myself an alcoholic; I didn't want the label. I don't identify that way even today. If I'm in a place where the social custom is to identify with that Twelve Step community, I usually identify as a *recovering* person. Outside of that, I identify as myself—whole, complete, resourceful, healed, continuously learning and evolving, and now available as a grateful servant-leader.

The Twelve Step recovery community ended my isolation. This is where I learned I wasn't alone, that there were people who truly had walked in my shoes and I in theirs, that they get who I am, how I'm wired, sober and otherwise. This is where I can learn that my experience can help others, especially women, who need to hear our stories. All our stories, all our voices. And in doing so, the shame that held me back from appreciating myself, from being kind to myself, that kept me trying to control certain aspects of my voice, my being, my soul from being seen, from being "too much" or "taking up too much space," all those things melted away in the power of service. None of the time I spent suffering as a child and during my years of addiction was wasted time when I put it to good use in helping others.

In the rooms of the Twelve Step programs, I've found so much laughter, real, honest, belly-busting laughter, the kind that leaves you crying and laughing about things that previously crippled me with shame. I've found friendships and joy in seeing others recover and get better. I've found tools for living that help me tolerate and embrace the experience of being human. And, frankly, it saves me from my hubris, from taking myself too seriously and believing my bullshit.

Most importantly, I've found faith in something still

nebulous but as real to me as the ground I stand on. I found it on the Eastern Shore of Delaware, in that quiet beach called Bethany, when I first imagined it on my bed in treatment. That sense of personal faith in something larger than life itself is the ground I stand on when I'm tuned into right. It's helped me solve practical problems; it's lifted the unstoppable compulsion I had to drink and use. While I don't practice or participate in any formalized religion, the Twelve Steps helped me understand that I had the agency and much-needed permission to develop a sense of spirituality outside of organized religion. It could be personal and meaningful to me. I also welcome what organized religion has to offer: community, spiritual guidance, principles, and thoughtful literature, which I welcome, read, and absorb. I found that, in my case, allowing myself to explore a more personal relationship with a spiritual life relieved my anxiety. It helped me create a new framework for living that I could use to examine my behaviors, my beliefs, and my feelings and exercise more intention and more choice about what I want out of life, how I want to show up, and what I believe is possible for me. It helped me find freedom from fear and crippling anxiety, like the panic attacks I would have driving in my town that would leave me suddenly feeling lost, like I didn't know where I was, what I was doing, or how to get out.

This journey has given me the space, time, and grace to accept myself, in all my fullness, in my changing body, my changing mind, my ever-changing emotions, and to forgive myself for all I've done, neglected to do, refused to do, or rebelled against. That became one of the cornerstones for how I choose to move through life, forgiving as much as I can each day for my feeble humanity. That doesn't mean that I don't embrace accountability, growth, or goals. But what that does for me is reset my ego and relax that anxiety-fueled and intense perfectionism that I could never achieve and what drove me to be so harshly judgmental and unforgiving of myself and others.

Coming Home to Acceptance

"Nobody, who has not been in the interior of a family, can say what the difficulties of any individual of that family may be."

—Jane Austen

"A dysfunctional family is any family with more than one person in it."

—Mary Karr

"It's not gender that makes a family; it's love. You don't need a mother and a father; you don't necessarily even need two parents. You just need someone who's got your back."

—Jodi Picoult

My parents are old and still alive as of this writing. My sister and I are fortunate to be witnesses to their sunset, the natural fading that comes for one's mind and body, should one be lucky enough to live that long. My dad always joked that if he'd known he would live into his eighties, he would have taken better care of himself when he was younger.

After so many years of struggle in our relationship, my mother and I have carved out one that works astonishingly well. Therapy, long years of therapy, writing letters that were never sent, and becoming a mother myself helped me let go of what happened in my childhood. I just got to a place where I couldn't carry the anger anymore—the anger she directed at me when I was so young, the control, misplaced attempts at humor that cut me deeply, all based on her own fears. The more I appreciated how each experience I went through shaped me and helped me grow into my own agency and self, the more I realized she could no longer harm me. I used the emotional memory of those years to help inform the intentional design of the family I wanted to create with my children and the values I wanted to honor with them. None of my past was wasted time; it all became useful in real, practical ways. As I learned to embrace my humanity and forgive myself, I forgave her and fell in love with her.

While my mother was an obvious antagonist in my early years, I accepted that my father did not protect me from my mother's anger and verbal and emotional abuse. At my father—workaholic, problem drinker, perhaps somewhere on the spectrum of alcoholism that runs so rampantly through his genetic line, a master of denial, mild-mannered, soft-voiced, incredibly generous, kind, hardworking, sincere, sweet, and earnest—I discovered latent anger toward him that I later turned inward toward myself, I think. Like I had with my mother, I opened to learning more about his beginnings, what was meaningful to him, and how he became the man he was. Like my mother, his life had been filled with tragedy and neglect. Being the last of ten children, with a father with an explosive temper and a mother lost to alcoholism during his teen years, my dad must have internalized anxiety and fierce self-reliance. He used that to catapult himself out of a dead-end existence into a profession that provided him stability, financial reward, and purpose. Exploring the relationship I have with him and the spider-webby ways our generational anxiety and depression crept inside us all brought me again to a new awareness. It opened me to more forgiveness, and I forgave him, too.

With my dad and sister, 1969

Ancestors

In the end, though, I discovered that what I wanted was a relationship with my parents, regardless of all that came before and regardless of their issues, which truthfully aren't mine to understand or fix. I learned to protect myself, exercise boundaries, and be present. Most importantly, I learned that these very imperfect, flawed, complicated humans love me in their own ways, as I love them in ways I don't entirely understand. It's primal.

My life and relationships with my parents today helped teach and shape the relationships and home life I created with my sons. There was much I wanted to do differently and much that I wanted to replicate. There was much I came up with on my own and much I learned from my friends. I found a mission in parenting healthy men, and I believe they are. The world really needs healthy men. My sons are wonderful, kind, honest, principled young men, open to growth and deepening their self-awareness. They seek counsel from wise sources. They have integrity and humor. They talk about their feelings. They are interdependent in healthy ways. They are more than I ever would have dreamed of, and they bring me incalculable joy.

After the long stage of parenting young boys into young men was over, I bought a home for myself. It was a little, post-divorce, post-kid-rearing, downsized home, just for me. While I was sorting through all the things I had collected over the years, I thought back to that first little condo I rented from my parents in Alexandria and what I owned when I first moved in so early in my sobriety journey: a 1970s jelly trifold plastic lawn chair lounger I used as a couch, a lamp, a stack of books, my bed, record player, vinyl records, and a few things for the kitchen.

Where did the rest of this stuff come from? I wondered in astonishment as I downsized from a townhouse, just over 2,000 square feet, to a 900-square-foot condo. I gifted things I no longer used, clothes that fit the body I occupied years ago, and anything associated with a partner who was no longer in my life, with the exception of one painting. It was one we bought together, but I found it and chose it, and it still delights me today. I gifted duplicates, things that came in sets when I only used one. I emptied drawers and found things once cherished that had been hidden for years, ready for use in someone else's home. I danced in the large outdoor space that came with the condo under ancient arching holly trees. And it was glorious. Glorious to have recovered financially enough to pull off a home purchase on my own. Glorious to rid myself of things that no longer served me, including any limiting beliefs about what I could do and deserved. My heart is filled with contentment and gratitude.

When I looked around this new space, I was delighted over and over again by the photos of family and friends and art on the walls, artifacts from my recent travels to places near and far off, meaningful places: the lakes and woods of Reston, Virginia, the ocean around Galway, Ireland, the unspeakable beauty of Lamu, Kenya, the spaciousness of sky and ancient life of Maasai Mara National Reserve, also in Kenya, my grounding sand and sea at Bethany Beach, Delaware, breathtaking waterfalls and glaciers in Fjallsárlón, Iceland, and heat, history, and heart in Athens and Skala Eressos, Greece. My home became a place of healing, laughter, and light, filled with friends and treasures I truly valued—a place for reading, knitting, writing, putting together jigsaw puzzles, and making art. It was a place brimming with creativity, expansion within a small footprint. Easy to maintain. It was a place that reflected my values, spirit, personality, and dreams. It was my sanctuary. It was home.

My work computer was upgraded to a Macbook Pro. After working for years as a technical writer, I joined the management team and found I had a natural ability in the field of leadership coaching. My passion ignited the more I learned about the topic, and I soon completed formalized training and became a certified leadership and career coach. All my experience, from childhood to girlhood to young adulthood through middle age, combined with the education I've embraced, formally and informally, has been key to my offering as a coach. Because of all I've experienced, I understand how much people need to feel safe before they can feel okay to be honest. Withholding judgment and holding a clear, open space allows my clients and me to be vulnerable. For some people, this is the first time they've allowed themselves to experience that with a total stranger. In this space, healing can happen, and my clients can choose to heal themselves. Like me, I truly believe humans have an extraordinary way of healing from the inside out, given enough desire, willingness, honesty, and tools.

After working in a wide variety of roles and industries, from homemaker to day-care provider, secretary to proofreader to writer to manager, in the defense industry, in the nonprofit sector, government contracting, and software development, I've found what common denominator secured my success: work that aligns with my core values. Anytime I've run into trouble is when I fell out of alignment with those, and I've seen that happen with other leaders.

I believe that anyone can be a leader. Leadership begins with you and how you choose to create your life. When you are aligned—standing in your truth, invoking courage to focus on your purpose, deepening your awareness to understand the impact your actions and words have on the world, and then taking the actions to do the next right thing—that is the essence of true leadership. It isn't a title, and it isn't a salary. It is our voices and everyday actions, most of which aren't seen, glamorous, recognized, or rewarded, where leadership develops.

It can feel counterintuitive, taking the time and space to

think about this. How many times have I been in life situations where I barely had enough money to survive, worried about how I would buy the most basic food to get me through the day? Hardly a time when I thought, *Wow, I should consider how I'm leading in my life! Maybe I should study this.* But like that thought experiment I challenged myself with in my early twenties, when I examined and then divorced myself from what I called "negative consumption" for a year, investing in new perspectives can change the framework for what I believe is possible today in my life. It influences and informs the actions I take. The more I deepen my awareness of my thoughts and how they influence my decisions and reactions, the more opportunities I have to positively impact the world. This conscious awareness is another life-changing gift of my sobriety journey.

Do I think sobriety is the only way to become a conscious and positive leader? Certainly not! There are many other paths one can travel down. However, it was my path, and this is my story to share with you.

Becoming free from drugs and alcohol could have been where I chose to stop my development. It is for many. That wasn't enough for me, though. The way I was wired, apparent even in early childhood, kept me from feeling alive, contented, happy, and purposeful. When I dulled my senses enough to sedate the emotional pain and discomfort I felt, I also denied my ability to feel joy. This continued development offered me the healing to live a full and contented life, one I could share with others.

When I think back to the girl I was when I first grew up—the one who suffered from night terrors, who bit the sides of her fingers to keep from screaming or simply to feel when her body was numb, who continued to try to become something her mother would love or even like, who survived being broken down from having her spirit shredded from emotional neglect, abuse, name-calling, wild accusations, gaslighting, hands and tongues on her body, unwelcome things in her body, and who was so desperate for love that she did nearly anything she could, including things below her line of dignity, trying to navigate all of that while appearing normal and building this image of success but melting down with anxiety and crippled by depression—it's a wonder I survived. If I hadn't found the Twelve Step community, what would have happened to me? How would my story be of value to anyone if I kept it hidden, bound in shame? I lived the first part of my life not knowing where I fit, trying to be the girl I thought you wanted me to be, filled with self-loathing, rejecting so much of myself, being unwanted, unacceptable, and unlovable. The healing doorway I passed through when there was no place left for me to go was a Twelve Step meeting room, which offered this journey of spiritual discovery. It relieved me of the things I was rapidly killing myself with long enough to decide I wanted the journey more than I wanted to leave. I've learned that I need to be around others to learn how to be a person. Like my dog, who missed being socialized as a puppy, she learned to be a dog by playing with other dogs. I needed that same level of socialization. Twelve Step meetings are where I heard incredibly wise nuggets, pure gold, about how to navigate being a human. Things like "Maybe I should just let someone be right," "Maybe it's okay to stop fighting [this person] [this idea] [this point of view]," "Maybe I can just allow this to be, without trying to fix or change it," and "Maybe, just for today, I can accept my current circumstances *just as they are.*" These are thoughts that do not come to me naturally. I hear them from others, and they floor me—every time.

After all this time, I've realized there's also a huge grieving that comes with becoming clean and sober. There's a grief that comes with the loss of identity, people, tradition, enjoyment, pleasure, and meaning. There's grief even with coming to terms with losing purpose and direction or acknowledging what was missing. Everything becomes new, and we want to rush to the other side of that, but you can't; you must stay in the moment, stay present, and feel every nuanced nook and cranny of being a human. Nearly excruciating for some of us who don't like "feeling" or "other people," but what a salvation it is to know that you aren't alone, and you don't need to carry this alone or figure it all out by yourself. Some people really get how I'm wired in those rooms, and slowly, ever so slowly, they helped me feel safe enough to heal.

The decision I make every day to stay clean and sober and continue learning how to use the Twelve Steps opens up a multitude of explorations leading me back into my spirit, cleansing and healing my grief-filled emotions, laying a warm blanket of acceptance over the terrible memories that haunted me, lifting me out of the depths of depression, pouring a gentle salve over my anxiety-frayed nerves, and allowing time for me to create space inside myself for all of me, where all of me fit, in my heart. I found my home inside my being.

I found the Twelve Step program's promises incomprehensible when I began my rocky journey. Not only have these promises come true for me, but they offered me a new framework within which I can comfortably and contentedly live. The promises follow, as listed in the literature, paraphrased:

We will become free and happy, relieved of all shame

from our past. We'll understand that none of what we had experienced was wasted or lost time; rather, it's useful to help newer people on their healing journey.

We will become peaceful and understand how necessary serenity is for our souls.

Thankfully, we'll realize we've stopped being so obsessed with our feelings and become more interested in how we can be useful to others.

Everything, including ourselves, will change. We'll learn to welcome change and accept it with grace.

We'll lose the fears we had about other people; others will simply become our fellow travelers at worst and our extended family at best. Along the way, we'll lose fears around finances: the acquiring of money, the management of money, that sense of doom many of us secretly feel that somehow things will end disastrously.

We learn to trust our intuition and judgment and let go enough to understand that things generally work out the way they will.

Notice that there's not a single mention of alcohol, drugs, wine, money, gambling, phones, shopping, sex, or any other material gain or addiction. It doesn't matter, in the end, what brought me here. What matters is that I was willing to try being a little bit honest each day, eventually willing to do a bit of work. My mind opened, and the rest fell into place, slowly, without me even realizing it.

Things come up for me, still. As long as I'm still breathing, they still will. Memories and tiny voices from the past come up for air, asking for forgiveness, asking to be seen. Things that would have brought me shame, things I would have said, *I'm taking this one to the grave and not telling a soul*. They're welcome here now. I welcome them in, even though they surprise me, make me cringe at first, or feel a pang of stabbing fear in my throat when they first pop up. I remember to try to breathe, pause, and welcome them in to share their stories. Only in that way can I heal. When they come up, now I know I'll be ready despite what I feel. The world will still follow its orbit, filled with unthinkable tragedies and stunningly breathless gifts, but I'll be different: grown, grounded, able to join with ease, surrounded by universal love.

This is my story to tell. Come, tell yours too. We need your voices, all of them. The stories we tell are the stories of survival and beyond. They are the maps we use to find our places of thriving, the lights we hold out for each other. I was chatting with my friend who ended up choosing sobriety four years ago after a legal issue, and apparently, just us chatting casually in her shop during our appointments gave her the safety she needed to become more honest with herself about her relationship with alcohol. Many women are struggling, desperate to know they are not alone. If you're struggling, trying to look like you have your shit together when you're falling apart, I get it. I know what that's like. You are not alone. There's a lot of support for you. You deserve to be free from sadness, anxiety, depression, hopelessness, and despair. You deserve to be healed and free. Reach out to someone. Tell someone your truth, even if all you can muster is a single-word sentence. Much love to you.

Acknowledgments

This story of transformation was not one that was made solely of my own efforts. Flying solo was what got me into so much trouble—mentally, emotionally, physically, and spiritually. There are many, many incredible people who traveled before and with me as I transformed into the woman who became willing to share this story. Countless men and women, feeling they were on the verge of losing everything, paved a path to recovery and developed the resources I benefit from still today.

I have so much to be grateful for, from the simple presence of those who journeyed alongside me, the wisdom they've shared, and the support and encouragement they've offered. I would not be contentedly healthy today without their love and support.

I'm thankful for my team at Koehler Books—John Koehler, Miranda Dillon, and Catherine Herold—who believe our stories are important to tell.

Gratitude to Sherri Moore and Marisa Stevenson and the rest of The Bad Girls Club, made up of incredibly strong women from my childhood.

I have so much love and gratitude for my friends Kasey Crowe and Monica Mather, the bravest women I know. They always remind me of something I strongly believe: that all our stories and voices are needed.

To Betsy Ross, Kate Malliarakis, Melissa Valley, Charles, and Dr. K, who saved me over and over.

To Becky Robinson and Minette Norman, two powerhouse women who offered me support and kindness when I was deep in a professional pivot.

I am also very grateful to Sarah Bullen, Kate Emmerson, and my writing friends from across the world, who encouraged me to keep going and stay with the stories.

Finally, I'm wildly blessed and grateful for my sons, Ryan and Anton, who give me more than they'll ever know, my sister, Kimberly, and my parents, Chuck and Joanne, who taught me everything about love and forgiveness.

Resources

Crisis and Emergency Resources

Emergency Resources: 911

Crisis Services: 24/7 Crisis Hotline: 988 Suicide & Crisis Lifeline 988lifeline.org: If you or someone you know is struggling or in crisis, help is available. Call or text 988 or chat 988lifeline.org. Veterans, press 1 when calling

Crisis Text Line: Text TALK to 741-741 to text with a trained crisis counselor from the Crisis Text Line for free, 24/7

Alcohol and Addiction Resources

SAMHSA (Substance Abuse and Mental Health Services Administration) SAMHSA's National Helpline, 1-800-662-HELP (4357) (also known as the Treatment Referral Routing Service), or TTY: 1-800-487-4889, is a confidential, free, 24-hour-a-day, 365-day-a-year, information service, in English and Spanish, for individuals and family members facing mental and/or substance use disorders. This service provides referrals to local treatment facilities, support groups, and community-based organizations. Also, visit the online treatment locator or send your zip code via text message: 435748 (HELP4U) to find help near you. Read more about the HELP4U text messaging service.

Alcoholics Anonymous and Online AA Intergroup to get help now, https://www.aa.org/

Sober.com

Recovery dharma, https://recoverydharma.org/

Caron.org

Veterans Resources

Veterans Crisis Line: Send a text to 838255.

Vets4Warriors: 855-838-8255, call, chat, or email, 24x7 confidential peer support.

Sexual Abuse Resources

RAINN National Sexual Assault Hotline: 1-800-656-HOPE (4673)

National Teen Dating Abuse Helpline: 1-866-331-9474

The Trevor Project: 1-866-488-7386

Citations

Erickson, Mandy. "AA Best for Alcohol Abstinence, Study Finds." Stanford Medicine News Center, March 11, 2020. https://med.stanford.edu/news/all-news/2020/03/alcoholics-anonymous-most-effective-path-to-alcohol-abstinence.html#:~:text=A%20Stanford%20researcher%20and%20two,achieve%20sobriety%20than%20therapy%20does.

www.ingramcontent.com/pod-product-compliance
Lightning Source LLC
LaVergne TN
LVHW041919070526
838199LV00051BA/2666